GENTLEMEN AND PLAYERS

The history of
the Tunbridge Wells Bridge Club

OLIVER KINSEY

Oliver Kinsey

Greenman Enterprise

ACKNOWLEDGEMENTS

The surviving Book of Rules (1886) of the Tunbridge Wells Club for Gentlemen lists those who were members in that year, including 38 identified as original members, and the leather-bound Candidates Book (1872) contains the names of all those elected to the Club up to 1987; without these valuable records I would have been unable to embark on this project. However, this history relies heavily on personal recollections and family stories.

I am therefore extremely grateful to all those members and others who have kindly provided material for this book, and my thanks go in particular to John Harvey, John Lott, Madeleine White, Mike Griffiths, Heather Nettleton, Angela Hollins, Bernie Waters, John Murrell, Angela Tompson, David Reich, Sue Holden, Ethnie Hodgens, Jeremy Willans, Catherine Draper, Colin Wilson, Stephen Pierce, Brian Lippard, Vida Bingham, Douglas Millson, Francis Briggs, Peter Quinton, Robert Seeckts, Roly Warner, Brian Waters, Christopher Hall, Jim Page and Lionel Shields.

I am also indebted to Brian Crack (the Secretary of the Kent Contract Bridge Association), John Burns (the Secretary of the Portland Club), Jessie Newton (former Chairman of the Welsh Bridge Union), Peter Hasenson (author of the *British Bridge Almanac*), Chris Jones (author of *Tunbridge Wells in 1909* and Newsletter Editor of the Royal Tunbridge Wells Civic Society), Roger Bassett (author of the history of the football clubs in Tunbridge Wells), and to the Archivist at Burrswood, the architects Burns Guthrie and Partners, and the law firms, Cripps Harries Hall and Buss Murton, for all the help and information they have given me. I also wish to thank my bridge partners and friends in the Club for their support, the current Chairman, Brian Lippard, for kindly reading and commenting on my draft text, and my publisher Michael Harte and my wife for their patience.

Although I have written about a considerable number of members, past and present, many others (of course) have not been mentioned, either because I lacked information about them or had to draw the line somewhere. Some of the 'Gentlemean and Players' in the book were not members, but they nonetheless enhanced the lives and times of those who were.

Oliver Kinsey   September 2009

Set in Garamond 11pt and published by
Greenman Enterprise
Greenman Farm
Wadhurst
East Sussex TN5 6LE

Printed by The Ink Pot
Southbank House
Victoria Road
Southborough
Kent TN4 0LT

ISBN 978-0-9561768-3-7

CONTENTS

Acknowledgements
Foreword by the Marquess of Abergavenny

Introduction   1

Part 1   The Victorians
1.   1872   4
2.   The Founder Members   7
3.   The first elected members   14
4.   1886 - The Rules   19
5.   The origins of whist and bridge   21

Part 2   The Edwardians and World War I
6.   The early 1900s   26
7.   1908   30
8.   1909   33
9.   1914 - 1918   40

Part 3   Between the Wars and World War II
10.   The early 1920s   43
11.   1925 - 1929   46
12.   The 1930s   48
13.   1939 - 1945   55

Part 4   The post-war years
14.   1946 - 1949   58
15.   The 1950s - the Counties Club   63
16.   The 1950s - the West Kent   67
17.   The 1960s - the Counties Club   73
18.   The 1960s - the West Kent   75

Part 5   Mergers
19.   The 1970s - the Counties Club   79
20.   The 1970s - the West Kent   86
21.   The 1980s   92
22.   1990 - 2004   98

Postscript   103

Selected Bibliography   104
Chairmen of the Counties Club and the TWBC   105
Chairmen of the West Kent Bridge Club   105
The Counties and TWBC membership numbers   105
Index   106

FOREWORD

by The Marquess of Abergavenny

In view of my family's association since 1873 with the Tunbridge Wells
Club and its successors, I was very pleased to become the Counties Club's
second President when my uncle, the 5th Marquess, died in 2000. I am
also happy to introduce this history, produced to mark the 100th
Anniversary of the occupation of the new club-house in 1909.

I learned to play bridge at school but regrettably I have not found time to
play the game much since then. I have read this story with great interest
and feel that it provides a valuable link with our predecessors and a lively
overview of an elusive game. I commend it to readers.

The VIth Marquess of Abergavenny

July 2009

INTRODUCTION

The Tunbridge Wells Bridge Club was originally constituted in 1872 as the Tunbridge Wells Club for Gentlemen. It changed its name to the Tunbridge Wells and Counties Club in 1909 when it occupied the club-house where it still resides. On 30 April 2004, it merged with the West Kent Bridge Club (founded in 1937) and adopted its present name. This book celebrates the Centenary of the club-house's opening - reported in the Courier on 20 August 1909.[1]

Signs of the times in the club-house were the electric lights duplicated by gas, and the "capital" view of the Common, much less wooded than today. The rooms for billiards, reading, smoking and playing cards defined the principal activities of the members. Who, though, were the gentlemen responsible for this new building, and how did it come into existence? The Club had had already survived for more than a third of a century, since the middle of the Victorian era. Who were its founders and early members, and what were their pursuits and distinctions?

This book seeks to answer these questions and to trace the Club's history from 1872 up to the date of the merger. The Candidates Book identifies the elected members and the 1886 Book of Rules names the Trustees and Committee in that year. The title deeds to 40 London Road and related papers refer to the relocation, and there are surviving minutes of committee meetings dating from 1919.

This is also the story of how the Club became a bridge club, and of the now-merged West Kent Bridge Club, running parallel with the evolution of the game of bridge during the 20th century. Bridge, originally a form of whist, had been associated with gentlemen's clubs in London since the 1890s. Auction bridge had been codified in 1908 and it had considerably wider appeal than the original game, then known as bridge-whist. Contract bridge was devised in the 1920s, followed by the duplicate version of that game which opened the way for public competitions. The number of people playing bridge in this country increased dramatically in the 1930s, largely as a result of books and magazine and newspaper articles and the publicity given to the game – much of which emanated from the USA, and the many bridge clubs and organizations which sprang up around Britain to promote the game.

Billiards and card games were played by the gentlemen members of the Tunbridge Wells Club from 1872, and the earliest record of bridge sessions being advertised in the Club is in the 1920s. A competitive bridge league was established in Tonbridge/Tunbridge Wells in 1932, and the Kent County Bridge Association was founded in 1937. After the War, the West Kent appeared to have an uncertain future and most of its members joined the Counties Club, which (looking to increase its revenue) decided to admit ladies as members. However, in the 1950s/60s (with its premises at 12 Boyne Park under new ownership) the West Kent enjoyed a revival and became one of the leading duplicate bridge clubs in the South East of England. Meanwhile, at the Counties Club, rubber bridge overtook billiards as the principal activity, and duplicate bridge was introduced during the 60s. The Counties merged in 1971 with the Tunbridge Wells Squash Rackets Club, but after three years the Squash Section withdrew and reverted to its previous separate existence. The West Kent had to leave Boyne Park in 1972. A merger with the Counties Club was one possibility,

---

[1] see text on page 36

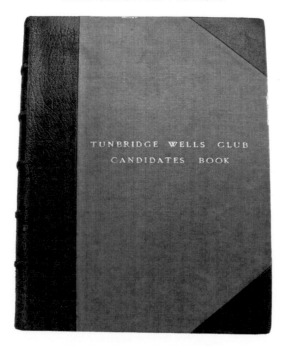

The Candidates Book of 1872

The first elected members

but for a number of years was not to be, even though the two clubs had many members in common. The West Kent's members played at the Masonic Hall until 1980 when those premises became unavailable. Since then (and for the last quarter of a century) they have shared the use of the Counties' club-house, but the West Kent retained its own management and separate identity until the merger in 2004.

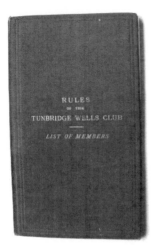 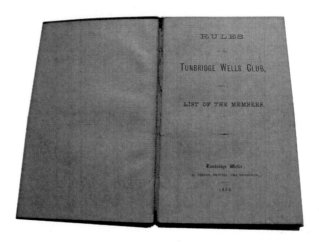

The Rules Book of 1886

This history describes several generations of members and others who have made significant contributions to the games of whist and bridge. It covers a period which witnessed two World Wars, great political, social and economic developments, and changing attitudes – from the days when Britain "ruled the waves" and the country was gripped by the Victorian class system - to today's world of computers. The activities of the members of these Clubs reflect the changing pattern of life in Tunbridge Wells, and the club-house has played a significant part in their lives. For some it has been a "home from home".

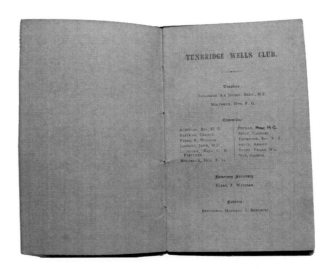

The Club's Officers and Committee 1886

- 1 -

1872

1872 was a year to remember. On 2 October at 11.26am precisely (time being of the essence), at the Reform Club, Phileas Fogg made a famous wager - of one half of his means. He was suitably engaged at that moment in one of his two occupations - playing whist with three of his fellow members, the other being to read the newspapers, essential before the appearance of 'the wireless'. This was of course the setting for Jules Verne's classic novel, *Around the World in 80 Days*, which was published as a serial in that year.

One of the leading newspaper stories of 1872 related to the events of 27 February when Queen Victoria took part in a public event for the first time since the death of her husband, Prince Albert, 11 years earlier. Large crowds lined the streets of London to see the procession in which the Queen rode in an open carriage on the way to a service at St Paul's Cathedral to give thanks for the return to health of her son, the Prince of Wales (later to be King Edward VII). Edward had been dangerously ill with typhoid fever, the disease which had killed his father. The congregation included the leading members of London society and politicians including the Prime Minister William Gladstone (1809-1898), a leading member of the Reform Club, who had instigated the celebration, and his great rival, Benjamin Disraeli (1804–1881), the Queen's favorite, who had been Prime Minister briefly in 1868. Disraeli was emerging from a period of political hibernation, and was to win the next General Election, dedicating himself to upholding the British Empire and improving the condition of England. He received the loudest cheers when he emerged from St Paul's, and he proceeded to the Carlton Club (then in Pall Mall) for a luncheon with his Tory colleagues.[2]

Gentlemen's clubs

Gentlemen's clubs, derived from coffee or chocolate houses, proliferated then in London as meeting places for the aristocracy and men of affairs. The Carlton Club was founded in 1832 as a party political organization whose primary object was to fight the supporters of the Reform Bill and to serve as a rallying point for the Tories after their defeat in the elections. The Reform Club was founded in 1834 when Brooks's refused to take new members, and all candidates were required to subscribe to the Reform Act of 1832.

Whilst the Reform and Carlton Clubs were mainly political, other clubs were formed for members of the armed services, or were sporting, university, theatrical, gambling, or purely social clubs. White's, the first, founded in 1693, produced every Prime Minister from Sir Robert Walpole to Sir Robert Peel and commissioned fine works of art. It also had young members who lost their money gambling and fought duels. Boodle's and Brooks's were founded in the 1760s. The Guards Club, believed to have been the first gentlemen's club to be owned by its members, was founded in 1810 as a result of the Peninsular War. London then had an influx of officers on leave or awaiting posting, and the Prince Regent and the Duke of Wellington were concerned that they should have somewhere inexpensive and respectable to stay. The members of the Marylebone

---

[2] Richard Aldous, *The Lion and the Unicorn*, Pimlico, 2007, p.218

Cricket Club (founded in the 18th century) played their first match at Henry Lord's ground in 1814, and London clubs flourished in the peace which followed the Battle of Waterloo.

The Portland Club

The Portland Club was founded in 1816 as the Stratford Club at Stratford Place, a house belonging to the Duke of Portland; it was reconstituted in 1825 as the Portland Club. It became the *alma mater* of whist and bridge in the same way as the MCC did in respect of cricket. The activities of the Portland Club and a number of its members are described below.

Tunbridge Wells

Outside London, towns such as Tunbridge Wells were expanding in the 1870s assisted by the advent of the railways in the 1840s and a growing birthrate. Since 1835 the town's government had consisted of a Board of Commissioners who were responsible under an Act of Parliament for lighting, policing, cleansing and otherwise improving the town, and for regulating the supply of water and establishing a market. In 1860 the Local Act was amended and the Improvement Commissioners were reconstituted – although the town did not become an incorporated Borough until 1889. The end of the 1860s saw the opening of the railway line to London via Sevenoaks, and by 1871 Tunbridge Wells had become a fashionable spa resort with a population of some 19,000 (35% higher than in 1861). According to the New York Times in 1874: *"the residents of Tunbridge Wells are severely respectable"*.[3] The town boasted spacious new houses designed by Decimus Burton which attracted new residents - including men and women of independent means and officers from the Army and Navy and former Government officials who had served abroad.

A memorable event in Tunbridge Wells in 1872 was the opening of one of the town's first public buildings – the Great Hall which included rooms for occupation by a new club for gentlemen, modeled on the clubs in London. Prior to 1872 Tunbridge Wells lacked a building suitable for public events and entertainment. This need was met by the Great Hall, then the town's most expensive building. It was situated (where it remains today) on Mount Pleasant, immediately opposite the South Eastern Railway Station and backing onto Calverley Park. The Public Rooms Company, which was responsible for the building, had been incorporated with a capital of £10,000 contributed by investors, and the imposing building was designed by the local architect Henry Hickman Cronk. It contained rooms for public meetings, banquets, concerts and theatrical shows - leading actors were hired to read from the classics and later, after the invention of the cinematograph, it included a cinema. It also had two wings, one of which housed studios for the new trade of photographers, and the other Terry's Restaurant which later became the Clarendon Hotel, and there was a brewer's store in the cellars.

The whole of the first floor of the Great Hall (pictured below) was designed for occupation by a gentlemen's club. These premises consisted of "a comfortably furnished club-room, card room, billiard room, reading room and other conveniences usually to be had in a first-rate club-house".[4] This was to be a social centre for the town's politicians and other leading gentlemen where they could enjoy each other's company, discuss the issues of the day, read newspapers and play billiards and cards. *"By incorporating the Tunbridge Wells Club for Gentlemen in the original design of the Great Hall,*

---

[3] Chris Jones, *Tunbridge Wells Civic Society Monograph No 10*, 2009
[4] J Radford Thomson, *Pelton's Illustrated Guide to Tunbridge Wells*, 1888

the Public Rooms Company ensured that the Grand Opening Concert would, indeed, be, under the distinguished patronage of the Nobility of the Neighbourhood."[5]

The Great Hall 1872

The founder members of the new Club (of whom there were some 38) celebrated its opening with a grand luncheon held on Wednesday 10 April 1872 – just six weeks after the Royal celebration at St Paul's. The opening luncheon was an important occasion for the leader of the town's government, the Honourable Francis George Molyneux, and was referred to in his obituary as one of the highlights of his life.[6]

From October 1872 the Club's members were kept informed of local events by a newly established newspaper, the Kent and Sussex Courier, which has continued to this day.

[5] David Peacock, *Tunbridge Wells Sketchbook*, 1978, p.8
[6] Kent and Sussex Courier 28 May 1886

THE FOUNDER MEMBERS
The Hon Francis Molyneux

The Honourable Francis Molyneux (1805-1886) was one of the main investors in the Great Hall who founded the Club and became one of its original Trustees. He was (at 67) apparently still in his prime, but the other Founders were surprisingly young. Julian Goldsmid MP, who became a baronet in 1878 (and was the other Trustee in 1886), was 34. Frederick Wadham Elers, the Club's first Honorary Secretary, was 39. Thomas Fox Simpson 45, John Stone-Wigg 44, Charles Robert Fletcher Lutwidge 37, and Frank William Stone – only 31. Molyneux, Elers, Fletcher Lutwidge and Stone became members of the Committee charged with the management of the Club; Simpson, Stone-Wigg and Fletcher Lutwidge became outstanding politicians of Tunbridge Wells and they are honoured by their portraits which hang today in the Council Chamber of the Town Hall.

Molyneux was the son of the 2nd Earl of Sefton. He had moved to Tunbridge Wells in the 1850s after Government service abroad. The Molyneux family was long established and influential in Lancashire, descended from a follower of William the Conqueror, with a stately home at Croxteth Hall. Francis was born in London at his father's house in Arlington Street, where he grew up with nine elder siblings, three brothers and six sisters. 10 years old at the time of the Battle of Waterloo, he was then educated at Charterhouse before going up to Trinity College, Cambridge. His obituary records that, *"being a contemporary of the old dueling days … he did not escape the ordeal of calling an opponent out"*[7]. Fortunately he survived. In 1827 (during the reign of King George IV) Molyneux joined the Foreign Office and worked in the administrations of the Duke of Wellington, Earl Grey, Viscount Melbourne and Sir Robert Peel. From 1835-1847 he was the Secretary of the British Legation in Frankfurt. In 1852 he would doubtless have attended the State Funeral of the Duke of Wellington, and been in awe of the country's great leader.

Molyneux's father, Lord Sefton, had a seat in the House of Lords and was known as "Lord Dashalong" because of his fondness for driving a carriage and four; he enjoyed field sports - particularly steeplechasing and hare coursing. He granted a lease of family land at Aintree to found the famous steeplechase course, and laid its Foundation Stone in 1829 (when his son Francis was 24 years old). Horses from the Sefton stables frequently competed in the Grand National. Lord Sefton and his eldest son (who became the 3rd Earl) also founded the Waterloo Cup (hare coursing's premier event) which was won several times by Sefton dogs. By 1855, though, Francis's father and all his siblings (bar one of his sisters) had died, but the earldom passed to his 20 year old nephew who became the 4th Earl.

Francis Molyneux and his wife Lady Georgiana Ashburnham, after returning from Germany, moved to Rochester. They then made some annual visits to Tunbridge Wells and rented properties such as the historic Gibraltar Cottage on the Common before purchasing the appropriately named Earl's Court on Mount Ephraim when its owner, Mrs Tighe, died. He had the house demolished and re-built and he and his wife and 10 year old daughter Constance took up occupation in 1858. He sat on the Bench as a Magistrate and was also a Director of the Oxted and Groombridge Railway. In 1860, the year of the new Local Act, he became one of the first of

[7] The Kent and Sussex Courier 28 May 1886

7

Tunbridge Wells' new Improvement Commissioners. Two years later he was elected Chairman of their Board - the town's governing body, and he was re-elected Chairman every year until his retirement in 1876.

Molyneux was much involved in the planning of the Great Hall including the rooms designed for the Tunbridge Wells Club for Gentlemen. The Club could hardly have found a more suitable person to become one of its first Trustees - known for his wise judgment and *"the courtly yet genial manner and the fund of humour and anecdotes which he displayed"*.[8] He made frequent public addresses, including in all probability one at the Club's opening luncheon, and a speech of welcome on behalf of the town to HRH Princess Louise when she laid the foundation stone of the Friendly Society's Hall.

Sir Julian Goldsmid Bt

Sir Julian Goldsmid Bt (1838-1896) was educated at University College, London and called to the Bar at Lincoln's Inn in 1864. He married Virginia Philipson and they had eight daughters. His uncle, Sir Francis Henry Goldsmid Bt, was the first Jew to become an English barrister, and his family established a reputation campaigning for the lifting of restrictions on Jews, Catholics and other non-Anglicans to enable them to enter the professions. Julian followed in his uncle's footsteps by joining the Bar. He practised on the Oxford Circuit for several years before becoming the Member of Parliament for Honiton in 1866 - aged 28, and from 1868-1875 he lived at 49 Grosvenor Street in Mayfair. After the Honiton constituency was disenfranchised he was elected for Rochester and held that seat for 10 years from 1870. He succeeded to his uncle's baronetcy in 1878. In 1885 he was elected for St Pancras and held that seat until his death, and also became Deputy Speaker in the House of Commons. He was a Director of the London Brighton and South Coast Railway, and the steam engine "Julian" was named after him in 1892. He was also a Magistrate and a Deputy Lieutenant for Kent, Sussex and Berkshire. He owned a number of fine homes, including Somerhill (where annual social and political events were held) and Nizels in Hildenborough. His family developed the Wick Estate in Hove, where roads bear their names, and where he died. He spoke at functions in New York, and his obituary in the New York Times described him as *"one of the wealthiest, most charitable, and best-known Hebrews in England"*.[9] Having no male heirs, Sir Julian's entailed property passed to his relative, Sir Osmond Elim D'Avigdor, who added the Goldsmid name to his.[10]

Thomas Fox Simpson

Thomas Fox Simpson (1827-1894) was born and grew up in Norfolk and he too moved his residence to Tunbridge Wells. In 1851 he enrolled there as a solicitor joining the partnership of Messrs Stone and Wall, which became Stone, Simpson and Wall. His legal practice became closely involved with the town's Local Board and he dealt with issues relating to the town's water supply. He also drafted the town's first building regulations and applied himself to the formation of polling districts for elections. He also promoted the town's first Fire Brigade which was manned by volunteers. Between 1870 and 1872 he was involved professionally, with his partner Frank William Stone, in the development of the Great Hall. As both were prominent solicitors, one of them probably did the legal work in connection with the foundation of the Club – but there are no

[8] Kent and Sussex Courier 28 May 1886
[9] New York Times 8 January 1896
[10] Sir David Lionel Salomons also then assumed Sir Julian's surname (see p.18)

known surviving records. Simpson became the town's first Magistrates' Clerk. His legal advice to the lay Magistrates must have been reliable because none of their decisions was apparently reversed on appeal. Later, in 1884, he became President of the Kent Law Society. He was also President of the Town Debating Society which met weekly in the Pump Room and Vice-President of the Literary Society for many years. His services as a reciter at public "penny readings" were much in demand. As recorded in his obituary: "*he was hand and glove and heart and soul in anything that appertained to the welfare of Tunbridge Wells.*" His voice must have been resonant and impressive because, as the Courier recorded: "*He did not disdain to adorn his oratory with a classical quotation from his beloved Horace ... describing himself (in Horace's words) as a man who shunned delights and lived laborious days*".[11] His portrait in the Town Hall clearly depicts a fine gentleman. He was survived by 10 of his 13 children, including Alfred Thomas Simpson who succeeded him as Magistrates' Clerk and was to play a major role in the Club's history.

John Stone-Wigg

John Stone-Wigg (1828-1897) became the leader of the town's government in 1878 when he was appointed Chairman of the above-mentioned Local Board - not long after the retirement of Molyneux. He was interested in providing open spaces for healthy recreation and in 1885 he took steps to create what was to become the town's first purpose-made municipal park, the Grosvenor Recreation Ground.[12] Stone-Wigg had previously been opposed to incorporating the town's government, fearing that that would lead to corruption, but, in 1888, having evidently changed his mind, he called a special meeting proposing that a petition be prepared to the Privy Council for a Charter for Incorporation. This was duly granted in January 1889, making Tunbridge Wells a Municipal Borough. Stone-Wigg became the first Charter Mayor, and served for three years as Mayor and as the town's Chief Magistrate. He paid the legal costs himself to obtain the Charter, arranged the design of armorial bearings for the new authority, and presented the mayoral chain of office. When he died he left part of today's Grosvenor Recreation Ground to the town and his children financed the purchase of the town's second recreation ground (St John's) in his memory.

Frederick Wadham Elers

Frederick Wadham Elers (1833-1917) was born in Ightham and educated at Tonbridge School, where he was a sportsman and particularly enjoyed his cricket. He graduated from Trinity College, Oxford, having played cricket for his college, and coxed the Oxford VIII twice in the Boat Race in the 1850s. After university, he continued to take a keen interest in sports. His home in Tunbridge Wells was at Manor Lodge, Bishops Down. "*He succeeded to an ample fortune when his father died which enabled him to devote himself to a life of public usefulness*".[13] However he was never married.

It was at a cricket lunch in a tent on the Common in 1868 that someone asked Elers the question - *why is there no Masonic Lodge in the town?* Elers agreed to see if the necessary number of signatures could be obtained to found a Lodge. He secured the agreement of Viscount Holmesdale to his name being used for the title of the Lodge, and found a sufficient number of backers, and the Holmesdale Lodge became the town's first Masonic Lodge, based in the Pump Room. He also

---

[11] Kent and Sussex Courier 21 September 1894
[12] Ian Beavis, author of chapter 11 of John Cunningham, *400 Years of the Wells*, Royal Tunbridge Wells Civic Society, 2005, p.124 *et seq*
[13] Kent and Sussex Courier 23 March 1917

organized major social events such as the annual Bachelors' Ball, amateur theatricals and athletics meetings, and was Secretary of the West Kent Foxhounds.

In 1872 Frederick Elers became the Club's first Honorary Secretary, and would have been much involved in the formation of the Club and the arrangements for its opening. He held that office and (it can be assumed) was responsible on a voluntary basis for the day to day management of the Club for the next 36 years. His name appears frequently in the Candidates Book as the proposer of prospective new members, and the fact that almost all the candidates were elected indicates that he conducted the process with good judgment and all due care and attention.

Elers founded the famous Blue Mantles Cricket Club in the 1860s. He would have been delighted by the success of a young gentleman (18 years his junior) who (like Elers) was an Oxford man. He was George Canning (1851-1932), better known as the 4th Lord Harris. Harris won a cricket "blue" and became the Kent County captain in 1871 and was the county's captain and leading player from then until 1889. He also captained England and became President of the MCC.

Another contemporary of Elers and cricketing friend of Harris was "the Great Cricketer" and best known Englishman of his time - Dr William Gilbert Grace (1848-1915). Harris and "WG" were members of the all-amateur team which toured Canada and North America in 1872. WG, who was also a champion 440 yards hurdler and a bowls player, invented modern batting and dominated the game of cricket for some 40 years. His first class career lasted from 1865 to 1908 and he helped the amateurs ("the Gentlemen") beat the professionals ("the Players") in most of those years. His top score was 344 for the MCC against Kent at Canterbury in 1876.

Cricket was and remained more than a topic of conversation at the Tunbridge Wells Club. One Saturday in July 1873, the Club promoted a match on the Common - the Bats v the Broomsticks, and it can be assumed that Elers was the principal organizer. He opened the batting for the Broomsticks and hit a six before being run out for 16.[14] His stay at the crease was short, but the coverage it received in the local newspaper suggests that it was entertaining.

One of Elers' greatest interests was in Tunbridge Wells' General Hospital, then in Grosvenor Road. He became its Treasurer and later Chairman, and wrote its history. Over a period of some 20 years hardly a day is said to have passed when he was not there to work or to visit and talk to in-patients, which he did in particular on Sunday afternoons and on Christmas Day. He delighted in the generous gifts made to the hospital by Sir David Lionel Salomons Bt, another member of the Club.

Elers served on the Bench as a Magistrate for many years and the cases which came before him were reported in detail by the local newspapers. His retirement as Honorary Secretary of the Club and his year as Mayor in 1909/1910 are described below.

Major Charles Fletcher Lutwidge

Major Charles Robert Fletcher Lutwidge (1835-1907) was the son of the Reverend Charles Lutwidge of Holmrook, Cumberland. He was the cousin of Charles Lutwidge Dodgson, better known as the author of 'Alice in Wonderland' - Lewis Carroll. Fletcher Ludwidge came to Kent at

---

[14] Tunbridge Wells Gazette 1 August 1873. There is nothing in that article to suggest that those playing for the Broomsticks used cut-down bats, but this was sometimes the case – W G Grace agreed to bat with a "broomstick" and scored 35 runs playing against F. Townsend's XI in 1874

the age of nine when his father accepted a living, but retained the family home in Cumberland. Charles (who remained unmarried) lived at Shandon, close to St James's Church where he became a Churchwarden. He remembered the Iron Duke and recounted that he had attended his funeral, when he would have been just 17. After graduating from university he was one of the first to join the Volunteer Corps, the Tunbridge Wells Corps of the Kent Rifle Volunteers. He apparently made a quick impact because he was promoted from Private to Corporal to Sergeant to Ensign in the space of a single evening, but he remained a volunteer until being gazetted as a Major.

In 1872 he was involved in the development of the Great Hall, and was a Committee Member of the Club. In 1877 he founded the Tunbridge Wells Centre of the St John's Ambulance Association. He became a Magistrate, and was one of the founders of the Volunteer Fire Brigade and of the Salvage Association; he presided over the Tunbridge Wells Harriers and was President of the Cygnus Swimming Club. He was also a talented artist and he used to paint landscapes on foreign travels and to show these and talk about his experiences at public entertainments which he organized for charitable purposes at Shandon.

In 1895 the town's Councillors found themselves in difficulty finding a suitable person to replace Sir David Salomons Bt as Mayor of Tunbridge Wells following the latter's very successful year in office. Sir David had not been an elected Councillor and the other members of the Council prevailed on Charles – "the Major", as he was known - to succeed him. He agreed, and did so well that he was asked to continue as Mayor for two more years - until 1898. One of the high points of his mayoralties was Queen Victoria's Diamond Jubilee in 1897 when he laid the foundation stone of the Indoor Swimming Bath in Monson Road. He was Mayor again in 1901-02 during which term of office he put on a spectacular firework display to celebrate the Coronation of King Edward VII. In 1903 he was honored by being made the first Freeman of the Borough.

Frank William Stone

Frank William Stone (1841-1921) was born at St Helena on the Tunbridge Wells Common which his grandfather (who was Steward of the Commons' Freeholders in 1835) leased from the Lord of the Manor. His ancestor, John Stone, was an attorney in Tonbridge in 1798, and the Stones were one of the oldest local families. After passing his law exams and winning the Clifford's Inn Prize, Frank followed his grandfather and father in 1863 into the family firm of solicitors. In 1867 he succeeded his partner, Mr Wall, as Clerk to the Tonbridge Board of Guardians. Then, he was involved (with his partner Thomas Fox Simpson) in the development of the Great Hall in 1872. Also in that year he married Annie Elisabeth Andrews and they had five sons and a daughter. He too became President of the Kent Law Society. He held numerous offices in the town's government including Joint Clerk to the Justices, Registrar of Births, Deaths and Marriages, Registrar of the County Court and Bankruptcy Court, and Chief Magistrate.

In 1898, he became Mayor of the town and served for two years. He made a particular name for himself by enabling the Local Board to gain control over the Tunbridge Wells Common and safeguarding the public rights over that land against encroachment by a section of the Freeholders (known as "hog pounders") who wished to build on the land. This he did by obtaining an order in the High Court sub-dividing the original freehold and adding 35 new names (known as "pimpers") to the roll of Freeholders. He was one of the founders of the Nevill Athletic Ground, President of the Tunbridge Wells Football Club and a keen all-round sportsman. He was also a bass singer in the Tunbridge Wells Vocal Association, of which he was President. He was a Churchwarden at St James's Church and shared with Archdeacon Scott a great interest in helping the poor. He was also a Freemason and for nearly 50 years a member of the above-mentioned Holmesdale Lodge. His obituary records that he *"represented the best type of old English gentleman"*.[15] Twenty years after he died, his son, Neville (appropriately on the centenary of his father's birth) became Chairman of the Club.

Dr Blackall Marsack

Dr Blackall Marsack (1826-1889) was the elder of two Founder Members in the medical profession, who were (it is believed) the two leading doctors in Tunbridge Wells in the second half of the 19th century. He lived in Upper Grosvenor Road close to the General Hospital and was the Honorary Surgeon at the hospital for 24 years.

Dr Frederick Manser

Dr Frederick Manser (1843-1924) was the other. He was born in Rochester and received his medical education at Guy's Hospital. He moved to Tunbridge Wells to be House Surgeon at the General Hospital in the 1860s and went into partnership with Dr Marsack in about 1870. In the next year he married Jane Bailey and he also became a member of the Royal College of Surgeons.

Manser was only nine years old when the Duke of Wellington died, but one day in the 1870s an elderly lady, who had known the Duke and was to have a considerable impact on Manser's life, came into his surgery and became one of his patients. She had been baptized Mary Ann Leshley at Chichester in 1788, and was known as Madame Caballero, after marrying a Spanish aristocrat, Antonio Aureliano Caballero, in 1820. She had been a well-known society courtesan, and beautiful.[16] She is said to have had liaisons with military officers and been nick-named "Moll Raffles". However her most lasting association was with the Iron Duke, and it is believed that her marriage to Caballero was arranged by the Wellesley family to ensure propriety.[17] In any event Madame Caballero became wealthy and acquired a number of properties, including "Grecian Villa" and its substantial grounds in Tunbridge Wells. This property she devised by a codicil to Dr Manser who inherited it when she died in 1877. After members of her family had tried unsuccessfully to overturn the codicil, Manser sold Grecian Villa which was then demolished. On its site now stand several rows of terraced houses in Grecian Road, Buckingham Road and Norfolk Road, which were all built in the 1880s.

Dr Manser was the longest surviving Founder Member. He was a member for 52 years, and served for 20 of those on the Committee. When he died at the age of 80, his obituary recorded that he had spent practically the whole of his life in the pursuit of his profession. *"In the alleviation of pain and suffering no one could have displayed greater skill."*[18]

Frank McClean

Frank McClean MA, LlD, FRS, FRAS, MICE, JP (1838-1904) was a Founder Member who became a pioneering civil engineer and astronomer. He was educated at Westminster and Trinity College, Cambridge, and then became a partner in the civil engineering firm of McClean and

---

[15] Kent and Sussex Courier 7 October 1921
[16] She was a contemporary of the famous French courtesan Marie Duplessis who died in 1846 - immortalized by Alexandre Dumas (fils) (1824-1895) in *La Dame aux Camélias* – the inspiration for Verdi's opera, *La Traviata*
[17] The Reffell Family History: www.reffell.org.uk
[18] Kent and Sussex Courier, 9 May 1924

Stileman involved in projects relating to the docks and railways; he later became Chairman and President of the Institute of Civil Engineers. In 1865 he married Ellen Greg and (later) lived at Rusthall House; in 1870 (at the age of 32) he turned to astronomy, and in particular solar and stellar spectroscopic research. He set up an observatory at his home and discovered the presence of oxygen in the helium class of stars, and made other contributions to the advancement of astronomy for which he was awarded the Gold Medal of the Royal Astronomical Society. In 1880 he founded the Isaac Newton studentships at Cambridge and in 1894 he presented the Victoria photographic telescope to the Royal Observatory. The estate he left of £300,000 enabled his son Francis (born in 1876) to "reach for the skies", first in a balloon and then in an aeroplane (as described below).

Arthur Wellesley Ward

Arthur Wellesley Ward, another of the Founders, was the son of John Ward JP, MP (1776-1855) who in 1826 had acquired from Matthew Calverley 874 acres, mainly of farmland, which became the Calverley Estate and employed Tunbridge Wells' famous son, Decimus Burton, to develop it – and create the new style of formal and carefully laid-out houses which attracted the town's new residents. Arthur lived at Calverley Manor and at 40 Park Street, Grosvenor Square in London; he was one of the Trustee Patrons of St. James's Church, out of which the St. Barnabas parish was carved in 1881.[19]

---

[19] Entries from the Church of England Record Centre file ECE/7/1/57391/1 pt. 1
18 December 1880 – the third Patron of St. James' is Arthur Wellesley Ward Esq. of 40 Park Street, Grosvenor Square, London [the son of John Ward who developed the Calverley Estate]
4 January 1881 – a letter from Arthur Wellesley Ward states "I have no objection to the constitution of the intended District nor to the plan of vesting the first presentation in Mr. Pearson, and the Patronage in Keble College."

THE FIRST ELECTED MEMBERS

1872

The 1872 Candidates Book lists the gentlemen proposed for membership, their professions or occupations, their proposers and seconders, and the dates when they were elected. About 10 new members were elected each year during the 1870s. Most described themselves as "gentleman" but some stated that they were vicars, Army or Navy officers (mainly retired), doctors, barristers or solicitors.

The Rev H J Rhodes

The first entry, dated 11 April 1872, the day after the celebratory lunch, was that of the Reverend H J Rhodes of Abingdon Lodge, Beulah Road. He was proposed and seconded by two of the Founding Members, Dr John Johnson and Charles Reily, and elected three weeks later on 3 May.

Charles Morland

Amongst the first to be elected was a member of a long-established family from Westmoreland, Charles William Morland JP (1849-1926) who lived at Court Lodge, Lamberhurst.

Rear Admiral Thomas Spratt

Also elected in 1872 was Rear Admiral Thomas Abel Brimage Spratt CB, RN, FRS, FGS (1811-1888) of Clare Lodge, Ephraim Road.

Thomas' father, Jack Spratt, was a Master's Mate on the 74 gun *HMS Defiance* at the Battle of Trafalgar in 1805. *Defiance* was at the rear of Admiral Collingwood's line and engaging the French ship, *L'Aigle*, which had been damaged. Jack jumped into the sea, armed with a cutlass, and swam to the *L'Aigle*. He climbed up her rudder chain, and was in the act of hauling down her colours when he was hit by a shell which was deflected by his cutlass from his chest and passed through his leg. After being hauled back on board the *Defiance*, he persuaded the surgeon not to amputate his leg. He was promoted immediately to Lieutenant, but had to spend several months in hospital in Gibraltar in considerable pain. He later took charge of the Prison Ship *Ganges* in Plymouth, and his wife bore him nine children. On his 60th birthday he swam 14 miles from Teignmouth to Ore Stone off Brixham and back to win a wager with a French officer.

Thomas Spratt must (when he learned of his father's heroism) have counted himself lucky to have been born. Not surprisingly, he followed his father into the Navy at the age of 16. He was a scientist, who, after becoming a surveyor and hydrographer, mapped the Aegean for the Admiralty and was responsible for the development of cable-laying techniques in the Crimean War. He was decorated not only by the British Government with Baltic, Crimean and Turkish medals and the Alma Clasp, but with the Legion d'Honneur (Officer 4th Class) by Emperor Napoleon III. He retired from the Navy in 1863 and settled down in Tunbridge Wells.

1873

The Nevill family

The Nevills have played an important part in the history of England for several hundred years, and in the 15th century the family was one of the most powerful in the country. Its head, the Earl of

Warwick, was called "the Kingmaker". His daughter, Anne Neville (1456-1485) became Queen in 1483 when her husband Prince Richard of York was crowned King Richard III. Also in the 15th century, one of the family, Sir Edward Nevill KG, married Lady Elisabeth Beauchamp, the daughter and heiress of Richard Beauchamp, Lord of Bergavenny, who owned a large amount of land in the Weald.

Queen Elizabeth I visited the Nevills at Eridge in 1573, although it was not then their main residence. In 1606 the 6th Lord Bergavenny was the host of Dudley Lord North who, during his visit, discovered the Chalybeate Spring – and Bergavenny then sank the wells which were to give Tunbridge Wells its name and the health-giving waters without which the town might not have been developed. The Bergavenny title was changed by the 14th Baron to Abergavenny in 1734, and his heir, the 15th Baron, became the 1st Earl of Abergavenny in 1784. In 1787 the 2nd Earl built the neo-Gothic Eridge Castle. Then in the 19th century, the Abergavennys made substantial estates around Tunbridge Wells available for residential development and the parkland at Eridge provided ideal wood for the manufacture of Tunbridge Ware.

The Candidates Book reveals that Lord Nevill of Eridge Castle was elected to the Club in 1873. His forenames were not stated, but the name of Henry Nevill appears in the book in the following year as a seconder of another candidate (Lord Pratt) and so it is likely that the gentleman in question was Henry Gilbert Ralph Nevill (1854-1938) who in 1927 was to become the 3rd Marquess of Abergavenny.

Lord Henry Nevill

Lord Henry Nevill (known as Ralph) was the second son of the 1st Marquess (5th Earl) of Abergavenny. He was educated at Eton and made one first-class cricket appearance at Lord's in 1879 playing for his own XI against I Zingari, whose team included his elder brother Reginald, who became the 2nd Marquess. He gained the rank of Major in the Sussex Imperial Yeomanry and later became a Lieutenant-Colonel in the Territorial Army Reserves (formerly the West Kent Yeomanry). He succeeded on the death of Reginald in 1927 to the titles of 3rd Marquess of Abergavenny, 7th Earl and 21st Lord Abergavenny. He was married three times (first to Violet Streatfeild in 1876), and was twice a widower. He was Deputy Lieutenant of Sussex. Like his father, he was a fox-hunting enthusiast and continued hunting until the age of 84 when he died after being thrown from his horse.

The Nevill family was clearly happy to support the recently formed Club because the name of Lord Henry's younger brother, the Honourable George Nevill, also appears in the book as a candidate for membership. However he was then only about 17 years old and his candidacy was withdrawn.

Lord Henry's father, Sir William Nevill (1826-1915), had also been educated at Eton and he then took a commission in the 2nd Life Guards and became a Lieutenant. Later he gained the rank of Honorary Colonel in the West Kent Yeomanry and Sussex Yeomanry. He married Caroline Johnson who bore him 11 children and lived mainly in Yorkshire where he enjoyed hunting and other sports. In 1868, he moved to Eridge Castle at the age of 42 when his father died and he inherited his titles. He was not only a soldier and country squire, but also one of the original organisers of the Conservative Party. Disraeli (who became Prime Minister for a short period in that year) was a good friend of his and used to visit him at Eridge. His enthusiasm for the Conservative cause earned him the sobriquet, "the Tory Bloodhound", and a Vanity Fair cartoon depicted him in 1875 with that title and stated that he had *"considerable influence in the preservation of privileges in which the people of England retain confidence"*.[20] Disraeli, 22 years his senior, must have admired the easy charm and energy for which he was known.

In 1876 he became the 1st Marquess of Abergavenny, and in July 1878 he organized an event which was to celebrate arguably the defining moment in Disraeli's career. This was a formal reception at Charing Cross Station, bedecked with flags and displays by the Queen's florist, to welcome Disraeli home after signing the Treaty of Berlin. That treaty secured peace in Europe until 1914.[21] In 1886 the Marquess became a Knight of the Garter. He organized winter cricket on the ice at Eridge and on August Bank Holiday 1888 he hosted a gathering at Eridge Park of some 30,000 people representing over 200 Conservative Associations.[22] He became a JP for Kent and for Monmouth and was Lord Lieutenant of Sussex. In view of his other commitments it is not surprising that he did not himself become a member of the Club.

1874

Sir David Lionel Salomons Bt

Sir David Lionel Salomons Bt (1851-1925) was another young man elected to the Club in 1874. He was the son of Philip Salomons and Emma Montefiore of Brighton. He was orphaned in his teens and went with his sisters to live with their uncle Sir David Salomons Bt (1797-1873) at Broomhill. He was educated privately and at University College, London, and Gonville and Caius College, Cambridge, and in 1873, when he was about to complete his degree in Natural Sciences at Cambridge, his uncle died and he inherited his estate and title.

Sir David's uncle had been one of the founders of the London and Westminster Bank and the first Jew to become Lord Mayor of London and to be elected a Member of Parliament. Not surprisingly the Salomons were great friends of the Goldsmids. David had followed Julian Goldsmid, 13 years his senior, to UCL where they both read law. They both succeeded to the Baronetcies of their respective uncles, Julian four years after David. It was no surprise therefore that Sir David applied to become a member of the Club.

In the same year in which Sir David joined the Club, he was called to the Bar (although he didn't practice) and stood (unsuccessfully) as the Liberal candidate for Mid-Kent in the General Election when the Tories, led by Disraeli, were returned to power. His decision to stand may have been influenced by the death in the previous year of his pioneering parliamentarian uncle. He became a Deputy Lieutenant for Kent, and also a JP although he did not often sit on the Bench.

Sir David had a passion for scientific matters and he had learned as a teenager how to make and repair clocks and watches. He started a series of popular scientific lectures for the general public in Tunbridge Wells which included electrical experiments. He also loved all forms of transport and built his own tricycle powered by a large and heavy battery. However this damaged clothing and so had to be given up. He also invented a railway signaling system, built a fine stable block at Broomhill for his horses, and later "the horseless carriages" which he pioneered.

---

[20] John Cunningham, *The Origins of Warwick Park and the Nevill Ground*, Royal Tunbridge Wells Civic Society, 2007, p.34
[21] Richard Aldous, *The Lion and the Unicorn*, Hutchinson, 2006, p.286
[22] John Cunningham, *The Origins of Warwick Park and the Nevill Ground*, Royal Tunbridge Wells Civic Society, 2007, p.34

In 1882 he married Laura de Stern, a second cousin of Sir Julian Goldsmid. Three years later he stood again for Parliament, again failing to win the seat, this time St George's in East Kent. He was considered to be a "Liberal Conservative" with a "left centre" attitude, and his obituary suggested that the reason for his lack of success was that he was *"too intellectually honest to accept all the shibboleths of party politics"*.[23] In 1894 Sir David was persuaded to become Mayor of Tunbridge Wells - not an elected Council member, but approached because of his reputation and known ability. At his inaugural Mayoral banquet held in the Great Hall beneath the Club's rooms, 300 guests including the Lord Mayor of London sat down to a great feast.[24] This was regarded as the most prestigious event which had ever occurred in the town.[25]

TUNWM : 1987.403

Sir David Salomons'1895 Mayoral Banquet in the Great Hall
This photograph was taken by Joseph Chamberlain, using a magnesium flare

Also whilst he was Mayor, Sir David promoted England's first Motor Show in Tunbridge Wells. He had acquired a car, the second in Britain, from a Frenchman, Monsieur Armand Peugeot, and, as there were only a few motor vehicles in the country, he arranged for others to be brought over for the Show from France. Sir David's Peugeot (purchased for £270) was capable of 15mph, nearly four times the legal limit of 4mph, and so challenged the law requiring that motor cars be preceded by a man with a red flag and a trumpet. The Show opened British eyes to the possibilities and English cars soon appeared on the market. He later took part in motor races in Britain and on the continent. He also founded the Aero Clubs of Great Britain and France, presented a cup for a circular aeroplane flight and wrote a book on aviation.

Sir David was a most generous benefactor and his gifts to the General Hospital, including the first X-ray machine, gave it the enviable reputation *"of having the best scientific equipment of any similar*

---

[23] Kent and Sussex Courier 24 April 1925
[24] Alan Savidge, *Royal Tunbridge Wells*, Midas Books, 1975, p.168
[25] Kent and Sussex Courier 24 April 1925

institution in the provinces".[26] He spent much of his time in London, either commuting from Tunbridge Wells or staying at 49 Grosvenor Street, Sir Julian Goldsmid's former home which he acquired in 1889. He was a Director of the South East and Chatham Railway, Chairman of the County of London Electricity Company and a member of the Council of the Institution of Electrical Engineers; he also inaugurated Tunbridge Wells' first electricity supply system. His household at Broomhill was one of the first to have electric lights, irons and the telephone.

In 1899 (three years after Sir Julian died with no male heirs) Sir David assumed the additional surnames and arms of Goldsmid and Stern.

Sir John Shaw Bt

Another baronet who joined the Club in 1874 was Sir John Charles Kenward Shaw Bt JP (1829-1909). He had four elder sisters and a twin brother and his father died before he and his brother were born. He was educated at Eton and Merton College Oxford. His brother went into the Church, and he succeeded to his uncle's baronetcy when the latter died in 1857 and lived at Kenward Park Yalding.

1875

Lord George Pratt

Lord George Murray Pratt (1843-1922) the second son of the 2nd Marquess Camden was elected to the Club in 1875. His family, friendly with the Nevills, were also substantial landowners in Kent. Lord George was educated at Eton and in 1862 entered the Grenadier Guards in which he served for seven years gaining the rank of Captain. He then joined the West Kent Yeomanry. In 1879 he married the daughter of the first Baron Cheylesmore and in 1883 joined the 3rd Batallion of the Berkshire Regiment in which he served for 15 years before retiring when second in command with the rank of Major and Hon Lieutenant-Colonel. He was no longer a member in 1886 and probably resigned when he moved to Berkshire, where he became a Magistrate, President of the East Berkshire Conservative Association and a member of the Berkshire County Council. He enjoyed outdoor sports and hunted with the Garth.

1876

Rear Admiral Francisco Tremlett

Amongst the members elected in 1876 was another naval officer, Captain Francisco Sangro Robert Dawson Tremlett RN (1815-1897). He was the only son of Admiral William Tremlett and had served in a number of heavily armed wooden sailing ships, the last of which was *HMS Impregnable* (2,406 tons and 98 guns). He had retired from the Navy in 1870 and was promoted to Rear Admiral (Retired) in 1878. He can be assumed to have been a friend of Admiral Spratt.

---

[26] Kent and Sussex Courier 23 March 1917

1886 – THE RULES

1886 was the year in which the earliest surviving copy of the Club's Rules was printed. It showed the names of 118 members. The Committee Members listed were: Rev H G Allington, George Bartram, F Wadham Elers, John Johnson MD, Major C R Fletcher Lutwidge, Hon F G Molyneux, H C Puckle, Charles Reily, Rev R T Thornton, Apsley Smith, Frank Wm Stone, and Samuel Wix.

The Rules tell us about the Club and how it was run. It was essentially a members' club because the Rules provided for any assets to be distributed between the members in the event of the Club's dissolution. Admission to membership was by a ballot of members at 4pm on the first Friday of each month, unless there were less than 15 members present, in which event the ballot was postponed until the next month. Rule 2 provided that "One black ball in five (members) shall exclude". The Committee could accordingly keep a tight rein on admissions, and ensure that the Club remained "exclusive".

The admission fee was six guineas.[27] The annual subscription was three guineas, or two guineas for those residing more than five miles from the Club. Visitors could be introduced on a limited number of occasions provided they lived more than 10 miles away. The Club was open from 9am until midnight, or 11pm if no member was in the building at that time. On Sundays, however, and in line with Victorian tradition, the Club was only open between 2pm and 6pm and no games were permitted. The members' activities mentioned were reading newspapers, pamphlets and books, which were the property of the Club and could not be removed, and playing billiards and card games. Smoking was permitted only in the rooms set apart by the Committee for that purpose.

Those wishing to play billiards were required to write their names on a slate provided for the purpose and to play in rotation. This must have been a popular activity because Rule 23 provided that "No gentleman having possession of the billiard table shall be permitted to play more than two games of fifty or one of a hundred, unless with the consent of the Members whose names are on the slate." Further, the Committee was empowered to fix the amount to be charged for the table.

The playing of cards was governed by Rule 21, which provided: "Cards shall only be played in the room appropriated for that purpose. No game of loo or hazard shall, on any pretence, be played nor dice used in the Club, except for backgammon. No higher stakes than half a crown points shall be played for, nor shall any bet exceed five shillings. The Committee shall forthwith investigate and visit with immediate expulsion any infraction of this Rule." It is probable that whist was often played by members at that time.

The Hon Francis Molyneux

In 1886 the Hon Francis Molyneux died after a period of illness. He had been one of the Club's originators and he remained a Committee Member until his death. He had retired from chairing the town's government in 1876, but had continued his involvement with numerous projects and institutions, such as schools (particularly for the poor) to which he gave prizes and other gifts and

---

[27] Six guineas in 1886 was the equivalent of approximately £590 today, allowing for average annual inflation of 3.8% in the interim – Bank of England Conversion Calculator

the General Hospital of which he was a Life Governor. He was very generous to numerous causes and made gifts at Christmas to every member of the Town's police force and fire brigade. He would walk on the Common at Easter handing out sweets and oranges to children and he made the grounds of his house available for fêtes and parties. His comment that Tunbridge Wells was "*the best watched, best paved and best lighted town*" became proverbial. He is also quoted saying:

> "I owe and I always acknowledge I owe far more to Tunbridge Wells than Tunbridge Wells owes to me. I came here more than a quarter of a century ago for a few weeks only, and attracted by the lovely scenery in the midst of which our town is placed, I lingered on, and never could tear myself away. I found here the three most precious gifts this earth affords - health, enjoyment, and friends." [28]

In 1904 his splendid house on Mount Ephraim became the Earl's Court Hotel; more recently it was the headquarters of Reliance Insurance, and it is now converted into residential flats and called Molyneux Place – on the corner of Molyneux Park Road.

Alfred Thomas Simpson

Captain Alfred Thomas Simpson (1859-1934) the son of the Founder Member Thomas Fox Simpson, who had joined the Club in 1882, succeeded Francis Molyneux on the Committee. Alfred was born in Tunbridge Wells. He had been a pupil at Tonbridge School when the Club was founded, and after leaving school he trained to become a solicitor and joined his father's firm, Stone Simpson and Co., and also the Territorial Army. In 1886, aged 27, he became Chairman of the newly-founded Tunbridge Wells Football Club.[29] He was an all-round sportsman – and particularly enjoyed his cricket becoming involved with the Blue Mantles, and a member of the Nevill Ground Committee. He was also an enthusiastic yachtsman and a member of the Royal Thames Yacht Club.

---

[28] Obituary in the Kent and Sussex Courier 28 May 1886
[29] Roger W. Bassett, *Better Then Than Now, A History of the Tunbridge Wells F.C (Two Blues) 1886-1914 and Tunbridge Wells Rangers FC 1903-1940*, Greenman Enterprise, 2008, p.7

THE ORIGINS OF WHIST AND BRIDGE

Whist must be considered as the game from which bridge was derived because the latter adopted so many of its features. Whist evolved from the game of "Trump" or "Triumph", also known as "Ruff and Honours", which was played in the 16th century. Bishop Latimer, during a sermon in Cambridge in December 1529, made some puns on "hearts" being "trumps" to invoke the spirit of Christmas. In 1628 the Worshipful Company of Playing Card Makers was founded as one of the trade guilds of the City of London, and the importation of foreign playing cards was made unlawful in order to protect that trade.

The popularity of whist increased in the 18th century, largely due to Edmund Hoyle (1672-1769) who was a whist tutor to members of high society and who wrote *A Short Treatise on the Game of Whist* published in 1742 which became a best-selling book. During the 19th century members of gentlemen's clubs in London became captivated by the game. It is believed that its rules were first codified in 1864, when the committee of the Portland Club, which was regarded as the chief whist club, approved a code submitted by the Arlington Club.[30] Four members of the Portland Club were particularly prominent: Lord Henry Bentinck (1804-1870), James Clay (1805-1873), Henry Derviche Jones (who also died in 1873), and his son Henry "Cavendish" Jones (1831-1899).

Lord Henry Bentinck was the son of the 4th Duke of Portland, educated at Oxford, who is credited with inventing the first signal in whist in 1834 to legitimately exchange information during play. His idea was that the play of an unnecessarily high card followed by a low card (which he called a "Blue Peter" after the signal flag) signalled "pay attention – please lead trumps". He was a Member of Parliament from 1846-1857 and, after retiring, played world class whist at the Portland Club. In 1886 Bentinck was a witness in the first scandal to afflict the game when Baron Henry de Ros (whose title dated back to 1264), a close friend of the Duke of Wellington and a successful whist player, was accused of marking the cards at Graham's Club. De Ros sued one of the other members for libel and hired the Attorney General to appear for him, but the jury found against him.[31]

James Clay was an eminent and highly successful writer on the game of whist and was a leading member of the Portland's Card Committee which approved the rules codified in 1864.

Henry Derviche Jones was a surgeon and avid whist player who was the Chairman of the above-mentioned Portland Committee. He was also the father of the famous Henry Jones (1831-1899), known by his *nom de plume*, "Cavendish".

Cavendish was educated at King's College School, Wimbledon and qualified as an MRCS and practised as a General Practitioner before turning in 1857 to writing about games and sports. Cavendish was the name of the club behind the Portland where Jones met James Clay. In 1857 Cavendish (at the age of 26) devised a method of proving that whist was a game of skill, putting four good players against four ordinary opponents – and having the former hold the North-South cards at one table and the East-West cards at the other. They played a series of deals and he proved his point when the good players won considerably more tricks than their opponents. This

---

[30] Ralph Nevill, *London Clubs*, Chatto & Windus, 1911
[31] Alan & Dorothy Truscott, *The New York Times Bridge Book*, 2002, p.4

was the duplicate principle in action.[32]   In 1862 he became whist editor of *Field*, the original country and field sports magazine, and produced numerous treatises codifying and commenting on the game. His book, *Cavendish on Whist*, published in 1863, was enormously popular and ran to 30 editions. The full title ran to nearly thirty words "The Laws and Principles of Whist stated and explained and its practice illustrated on an original system by means of hands played completely through". In 1871 Cavendish became Secretary of the All England Croquet Club and in 1875 proposed that one of the lawns be set aside for tennis. The first Wimbledon men's championship took place in 1877 and he was the referee.

Whist was not surprisingly the subject of literary references during the 19th century: Charles Lamb described "Mrs Battle's opinions on whist" in an essay which may have reflected his own perception of the game:

> "A clear fire, a clean hearth, and the rigour of the game". This was the celebrated wish of old Sarah Battle (now with God) who next to her devotions loved a good game of whist. … She loved a thorough paced partner, a determined enemy. She took and gave no concessions. She hated favours. She never made a revoke, nor ever passed it over in her adversary without exacting the utmost forfeiture. She fought a good fight – cut and thrust. She sat bolt upright – never introduced or connived at miscellaneous conversation during its progress. Hearts was her favourite suit … As she emphatically observed "cards are cards" … It [whist] was her business, her duty, the thing she came into the world to do, and she did it. She unbent her mind afterwards over a book." [33]

Mr Pickwick suffered anguish after being inveigled into a game of whist with three imposing women in the *Pickwick Papers*.[34] George Eliot described the latter half of the day as being made up of "dinner, wine, whist, and general satisfaction".[35]

Edgar Allan Poe also commented on the game in the first "detective" novel: *"Whist has long been noted for its influence upon what is termed the calculating power, and men of the highest order of intellect have been known to take an apparently unaccountable delight in it, whilst eschewing chess as frivolous"*.[36] Jules Verne wrote: *"Phileas Fogg often won at this game, which, as a silent one, harmonized with his nature."*[37] Was this a hint that Fogg would deploy his superior intellect to win his wager?

It seems most likely that bridge originated in South Eastern Europe, and probably in Constantinople, either in the 1850s during the Crimean War or 1880s. John Collinson (1842-1922) of London wrote a letter to the Saturday Review in 1906 stating:

> "Between 1880-84 I spent a considerable time in Constantinople and Asia Minor where I played what was then called "Biritch or Russian Whist". I was then living, while in England, at Cromwell Road and introduced the game to many of my English friends,

---

[32] The duplicate principle was not widely adopted until 1891 when the American Whist League was formed, the Kalamazoo tray (the first duplicate board) was invented and the first book on tournament organization was written by John T Mitchell, who devised the first "movement" for pairs' play and the method of match pointing
[33] Charles Lamb, *Essays of Elia*, 1821
[34] Charles Dickens, *The Pickwick Papers*, published in 19 issues, 1836-37
[35] George Eliot, *Middlemarch*, William Blackwood & Sons, 1871
[36] Edgar Allan Poe, *The Murders in the Rue Morgue*, 1841
[37] Jules Verne, *Around the World in 80 Days*, 1872 (in serial form)

who liked it so much that they asked me to have the rules printed ... "Biritch" was attributed to the Russian colony at Constantinople." [38]

The word "Biritch" (of Serbo-Croatian or Ukrainian origin) may have been changed to "bridge" by British officers or civil servants in Constantinople, and there is a suggestion that the name came from the Galatea Bridge across which soldiers walked to the coffee houses to play the game.

In any event, Mr Collinson can be credited with having been the author of the earliest surviving rules of the game. This is a miniature book or booklet (dimensions five inches by three) entitled *Biritch or Russian Whist* which was published on 9 July 1886. It is bound between fairly hard covers and contains 28 sheets of paper, of which only four of the 56 pages have anything printed on them. The first two and the last 50 pages are blank – perhaps for notes or scores to be added.[39]

Mr Collinson's booklet sets out the rules of the game he had learned in Constantinople which at some point became known as bridge, but which, after auction bridge emerged in about 1903, was called "bridge whist" to distinguish it from auction bridge.

Bridge whist closely resembled whist, subject to three important differences – the ability of the dealer (or his partner) to call the trump suit, the introduction of a "dummy" hand (derived from "dummy whist"), and the introduction of the double/redouble.[40] Whist had been regarded as the "quiet" game (to which Jules Verne referred) - the trump suit was determined by the dealer turning up the last card to be dealt, and there was no necessity for the players to speak. Collinson's rules provided that no card should be turned up for trumps, but that the dealer should, after the players had looked at their cards, choose trumps. Alternatively, he could say either *"Biritch"* - requiring the hand to be played with no trumps, or *"pass"*. If the dealer passed, his partner was required to declare trumps or say *"Biritch"*. Either of the opponents could then say *"Contre"* (double), suggesting a French influence, and either the dealer or his partner could then say *"Sur contre"* (redouble). Further redoubles could be made - ad infinitum - doubling, quadrupling etc the value of each trick. The decision whether to double or redouble was quite a gamble because none of the players knew the distribution of the cards held by the others, and, depending on the number of redoubles and the size of the stake, a large amount of money could be won or lost on a single hand. This element changed the complexion of the game of whist by introducing a new *frisson*. The existence of a dummy hand face up on the table made the cards easier to play in bridge than in whist, and the whist-playing skills of the likes of Lord Henry Bentinck and Henry (Cavendish) Jones must be regarded as all the more exceptional.

Neither Mr Collinson's booklet nor the game it described seem to have become widely known in London for a number of years. He and his friends clearly enjoyed playing the game, but others who heard about it may have preferred to continue playing the "quiet" game. One place where one might have expected to find gentlemen attracted by the new game and its possibilities was the Portland Club. However, it appears that eight years were to pass before that event occurred.

In *Leather Armchairs*, his book about gentlemen's clubs, Charles Graves wrote:

---

[38] John Collinson, Letter to the *Saturday Review*, 28 May 1906. www.pagat.com/boston/biritch.html
[39] There are only three known surviving copies of this booklet, which are held in the Bodleian Library in Oxford, the Cambridge University Library and the Public Record Office
[40] Henry G Francis, *The Official Encyclopaedia of Bridge*, The American Contract Bridge League, Sixth Edn, 2001, p.45

"It is certain that the first game of bridge ever played in England took place at the Portland Club in 1894.[41] It appears that Lord Brougham entered the club after a long visit to the family villa in Cannes and absent-mindedly, when dealing the first hand in a rubber of whist, failed to turn up the last card. When the other three players expressed shocked surprise, he replied, "I thought I was playing bridge – the most fascinating card game I know, if you will let me teach you the rules. I learned it recently in France." The three players agreed, played a rubber and were most enthusiastic. Very shortly almost every member was playing the new game, in spite of the protests of Henry Jones, the great whist expert, who wrote under the name of Cavendish."[42]

Cavendish must have regarded the new game as a crude development requiring more guile and less intelligence. In 1895 Thomas De La Rue & Co published some laws of bridge with a guide to the game by Boaz. In the following year a committee of three of the Portland's members drafted a code and laws which were approved by a joint committee of the Portland and Turf Clubs and issued as the standard Rules of Bridge. In 1898 a treatise entitled *How to play bridge* was written by Badsworth, the *nom de plume* of another member of the Portland Club.[43]

More books followed – including William Dalton's *Complete Bridge*, first published in 1900, in which he wrote:

"Bridge has to a certain extent revolutionized society. It has shortened the long, weary and unwholesome dinners of ten years ago. It has altered the entirely tedious hour in the drawing room after dinner when one used to count the minutes until one could decently take one's departure. It has done away with the monotony of that awful wet day in a country house which we used to know so well: and it has given an added interest in life to many people."

Who were the first members of the Tunbridge Wells Club to play bridge? The answer is that there are no records to answer the question but James Lushington or Richard Limbery-Buse are likely contenders.

James Law Lushington

James Law Lushington (1823-1905) was elected to the Club in 1891 and probably learned the game of bridge travelling to and from India. James was born in Trichinopoly, Madras, and was a Magistrate and Collector in the Indian Civil Service before retiring to Tunbridge Wells.[44] One of his eight sons, Percy Manners Lushington (1863-1955), born in Calcutta and the father of John Lushington (referred to below) was a bridge-player who is believed to have learned the game from his father James. He (Percy) used to recount to his grand-daughter (Heather Nettleton) how in the

---

[41] This statement is of course contradicted by Mr Collinson's letter. It should also be noted that bridge whist had reached the USA by 1892/93, that Henry Barbey had some rules of bridge printed privately in 1892, and a letter published in *Bridge Magazine* 1932 states that Frank J.Nathan played a game of bridge at the St George's Club in Hanover Square in 1892

[42] Charles Graves, *Leather Armchairs*, 1974, p.32

[43] William.Dalton, *Complete Bridge*, Frederick A Stokes, New York, 1906
www.archive.org/details/daltonscomplete00daltgoog

[44] A relative of member James Lushington, Lieutenant-General Sir James Law Lushington (1779-1859), had been a dashing cavalry officer in India who became a Director of the East India Company in 1827 and later its Chairman

olden days James played bridge on board ships to and from India – where clever card sharps wagered enough money to pay their fares.

Richard B Limbery-Buse

Richard B Limbery-Buse (1861-1942) was elected to the Club in 1899. He read law at Cambridge with a view to practising as a solicitor, but his parents decided that, due to his delicate health, he should not work.[45] Later, he spent the winter months in Switzerland and let his house in St John's Road.[46] Bridge became his main interest, as described below, and it seems probable that he learned whist as a young man. His nature suggests that he may not have been attracted by bridge whist, and, if that was the case, one would assume that, like many others, he took up bridge after auction bridge emerged and was codified in 1908.

---

[45] Richard Cobb, *Still Life*, Chatto & Windus, 1983. Richard Cobb's mother was a cousin of Mr Limbury-Buse

[46] *Tunbridge Wells Society*, 1909

- 6 -

THE EARLY 1900s

The coronation of King Edward VII in 1901 marked the beginning of a new era. In Tunbridge Wells excited crowds turned out on the Common to watch Major Fletcher Lutwidge's celebratory firework display.

1903

It appears that by 1903 the Tunbridge Wells Club may have begun to investigate the possibility of acquiring land in London Road on which to build a new club-house. Five years later, when this became a reality, the existing rooms in the Great Hall were described in the press as "makeshift". Alfred Simpson (the Committee member and son of founder Thomas Fox Simpson) was a solicitor and he became involved as an agent in a transaction in 1903 to purchase part of the land which the Club was to acquire in 1908.

Also involved was Louis Stephen Beale (1853-1939), who was later to develop the property for the Club. Mr Beale was the town's leading builder. As John Cunningham relates in his book on the origins of Warwick Park, Mr Beale left school at the age of 14 and joined his father who was a carpenter in a builders' business.   His obituary records that, after going through all the departments, he became head of the firm and made many distinctive designs, and that his skilful work made many valuable contributions to the architecture of the town. He was a prominent Freemason and Prime Warden of the Worshipful Company of Blacksmiths, and in 1896 had been the President of the Tunbridge Wells Tradesmen's Association.[47]

Belmont Lodge and Belair Cottage

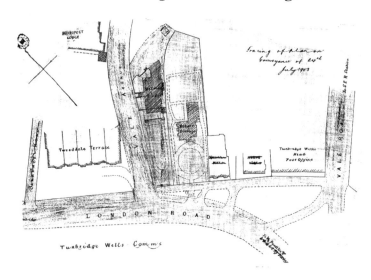

---

[47] John Cunningham, *The Origins of Warwick Park and the Nevill Ground*, Royal Tunbridge Wells Civic Society, 2007, p.43

There were then two adjacent detached dwellinghouses on the London Road which overlooked the Common, Belair Cottage (No 40) and on its north side Belmont Lodge (No 41); they were in separate ownership. Both houses were set back from the roadway; Belmont was larger and further back than Belair, but both had sizeable gardens.

Alfred Simpson (acting as agent for Mrs Ellen Kelso, a widow) entered into a contract to purchase Belmont for £1,770, no doubt for her to occupy herself. At the same time Mr Beale agreed to buy Belair for £1,225. Shortly afterwards, before either of these agreements was completed, Mr Beale agreed to sell Belair to Mrs Kelso for £1,255 – (ie at a very nominal profit). Belmont and Belair were then conveyed together by their previous owners to Mrs Kelso.

It is not clear why Mr Beale did not proceed with his purchase of Belair at that time but it seems likely that his purpose was to develop the property. He could have decided not to proceed for any reason, but the involvement of Mr Simpson and the events which followed five years later suggest that the collaboration between Mr Beale and the Club may have begun in 1903. Their idea then may have been to purchase Belair and also the front garden of Belmont (which Mrs Kelso may have been willing to sell). She may have changed her mind, or the Club's Committee or members may not have been sufficiently behind the idea, or may have been unable to raise the necessary finance.

In any event, the outcome in 1903 was that Mrs Kelso became the owner of both Belmont and Belair. However in March 1904 she died, and her son, Stephen, and unmarried daughter, Elizabeth, inherited her estate - the former receiving Belair, and the latter Belmont. The Club did not become involved until 1908 – in the years up to 1905 the man who was to take the matter forward and become Chairman of the Club, Henry Knipe, whose portrait hangs in the club-house, was involved in another daunting project – writing a history of the Universe.

Henry Robert Knipe

Henry Robert Knipe LLB JP FLS FGS (1855-1918) had been elected a member of the Club in 1897. He was the son of Mr E S Knipe of Queensgate, London S.W. and was educated at Harrow and Trinity College, Cambridge. He was a Barrister and a JP for Sussex and a member of East Sussex County Council. He had previously lived in Hove and he chose the Sussex part of Tunbridge Wells for his residence in order to preserve his territorial qualification for that Council.[48] He never married. He (like Frederick Elers) took an active interest in the General Hospital and was to succeed Elers as its Chairman and Treasurer. He also became Chairman of the Children's Convalescent Home, Chairman and Treasurer of the Broadwater Down Conservative Association, and President of the Tunbridge Wells Literary Society. He was extremely knowledgeable about natural sciences, and was a specialist in geology and flora and fauna.

1905 *Nebula to Man*

In 1905 Henry Knipe completed writing an illustrated history of the universe in verse which was entitled *Nebula to Man*. He must have been inspired by Charles Darwin (1809-1892), himself a man of Kent, who was well-known for his study of the origin of our species. In the preface Knipe wrote:

---

[48] Kent and Sussex Courier 7 August 1918

"*Nebula to Man* is an attempt to present a sketch of the evolution of the earth on the Nebular Hypothesis; to note also subsequent sea and land movements, and successive appearances of life, as revealed by the geological strata. ... To attempt a work of this kind in rhyme is, I know, a bold experiment. But, however severely scientific in some of its aspects, the story of Geology is truly the most enchanting story in the world."

His obituary stated: "*He had to bend his rhyming ingenuity to the exigencies of a severely scientific narrative.*"[49] The book begins as follows:

> A glowing mist, through realms of space unbounded,
> Whirls on its way, by starry hosts surrounded.
> Dim is its lustre, as compared with theirs,
> And more the look of stars dissolved it wears.
> Volumes of heat, from its prodigious stores,
> To endless space, it never ceasing pours.
> Formless and void it seems, and yet it holds
> A coming world within its hazy folds.

A later passage, quoted on the first page of the *Oxford Illustrated Prehistory of Europe*, concludes:

> Primeval men are now upon the scene –
> Short, thick-boned hairy beings of savage mien
> With ape-like sculls: but yet endowed with pride
> And power of mind to lower brutes denied.[50]

Henry Knipe produced several more books: *Evolution in the Past* was published in 1912, and a *Chronicle of Tunbridge Wells* for the period 1608 to 1915 was written by him for the Congress of the South Eastern Union of Scientific Societies held in the town and published in 1915. In 1916 he became the Tunbridge Wells Editor for the *Encyclopaedia of British Flora*.

The first Victoria Cross – Rear Admiral Charles Davis Lucas

In 1906 Rear Admiral Charles Davis Lucas RN VC JP (1834-1914) was elected a member of the Club – he was the third admiral in the Club, although the first two (Spratt and Tremlett) were no no longer alive. Charles was married to Frances; they lived at Great Culverden in a park of 100 acres on Mount Ephraim. The letters "VC" are written after his name in the Candidates Book, but the letters are small and can easily be overlooked. 52 years earlier, Charles (then a 20 year old midshipman) had been the first person to perform a gallant act which earned him the Victoria Cross, the nation's highest award for outstanding gallantry, at the Battle of Bomarsund in the Crimean War. It changed his life and later led to his marriage and retirement in Tunbridge Wells.

Born into a wealthy landowning family in County Armagh, Lucas joined the Navy at the age of 14. On 20 June 1854 he was serving on the new steam sloop *HMS Hecla* under the command of Captain William Hall. They were involved in an ill-advised and unsuccessful attack with two other ships on the heavily fortified Russian fortress of Bomarsund in the Aland Islands in the Baltic. The Russians had more than 100 guns against 38 on the British ships including only eight on the *Hecla*, which was designed for speed and reconnaissance work. A live shell landed on the *Hecla's*

---

[49] Kent and Sussex Courier 7 August 1918
[50] Henry Knipe, *Nebula to Man*, J M Dent, 1905

upper deck; a cry went up for all hands to hit the deck, but Lucas picked up the shell with its fuse burning, carried it to the rail and heaved it overboard. It exploded before it hit the water and two men were slightly hurt. Captain Hall promoted Lucas to Acting Lieutenant on the spot; the promotion was subsequently confirmed, and Lucas was awarded a gold Royal Humane Society Medal. Three years later he was invested by the Queen with the Victoria Cross. He served on *HMS Liffey*, *HMS Edinburgh*, *HMS Calcutta* and finally as Captain of *HMS Indus* before retiring (at the age of 39) in 1873 and going to live with his sister and brother-in-law in the Western Highlands.

In 1878 Charles Lucas's life changed again when he received a request from the dying Admiral Sir William Hall KCB - to look after his wife, formerly the Hon Hilaire Caroline Byng, the daughter of the 6th Viscount Torrington, and to marry their daughter Frances.[51] *"Lucas was an incurable romantic and he agreed".*[52] He married Frances in 1879 and in 1885 (still only 50) he was promoted to Rear Admiral on the retired list. He then served as a Justice of the Peace in Kent and Scotland and in 1909 he was Chairman of the North Ward Conservative Association. His home at Great Culverden was demolished in 1927 and the Kent and Sussex Hospital now stands on its site, and surrounding roads bear the Culverden and Byng names.

In 2006 Charles Lucas was honoured by being included in a set of Royal Mail stamps commemorating six of the heroic servicemen who received the Victoria Cross.

---

[51] Lady Hall was descended from Admiral John Byng (the son of the 1st Viscount Torrington) who was court-martialed and executed in 1757 for not doing his utmost against the enemy – when King George II declined to grant the clemency requested by the judges and the Leader of the House of Commons
[52] Brian Best, *Charles Lucas – The First VC*, www.victoriacrosssociety.com

7

1908

The acquisition of the site for a new club-house

On 6 May 1908 Elizabeth and Stephen Kelso conveyed their respective properties (Belmont Lodge and Belair Cottage) to the developer, Mr Beale, for the aggregate consideration of £3,150, (£1,863 for the former and £1,287 for the latter). On the following day there was a Special General Meeting of the Club's members over which the Chairman, Henry Knipe, presided, and at which they agreed to proceed with the acquisition of the site for their proposed new club-house. This was the front part of the Belair property (including the house) and the front garden/grounds of Belmont. The minutes of the SGM (which have been retained with the Title Deeds) speak for themselves:

> "The Chairman read an exhaustive Report on the Scheme prepared by Messrs Beale & Sons for the erection of a suitable Club-house on part of the sites at present occupied by two detached houses, "Belair" and "Belmont" in the London Road and to be leased to the Club for 28 years at a rental of £350 per annum with an option to purchase within two years for £7,000, of which Messrs Beale & Sons would accept £4,000 in cash and allow £3,000 on mortgage at 4%. It was resolved that this meeting approve of the recommendation of the Committee that, if the necessary financial requirements can be arranged, the Club-house be built on the site of "Belmont" and "Belair" according to the plans submitted."[53]

It is clear from the above that plans of the proposed development had been prepared and that there had been detailed negotiations between the Club and Mr Beale. The fact that the meeting took place after Mr Beale had acquired the property suggests that the Committee was more than confident that the members would approve its recommendation.

In July Mr Knipe reported that he had had a meeting with Mr Beale, who was willing to leave an extra £500 outstanding on mortgage, and in August the Club held another SGM at which the Committee was authorized to increase the mortgage to £3,500 and, if necessary to raise a second mortgage of £500 at 4%. In September Mr Beale submitted two estimates for the development, one using his own plans amounting to £7,122, and the other using plans prepared by a young architect, Cecil Burns (aged 25) practising in Lincoln's Inn Fields, amounting to £7,442. The members resolved to adopt the latter's plans provided Mr Beale would agree to carry out the development (including the cost of the land) for £7,300.[54] They also appointed Messrs Knipe, Simpson and John Gordon as Trustees; this was necessary to enable them to become the owners of the property and to hold it on trust for the Club.

Then in November the Committee authorized the recently appointed Trustees to sign the building contract and the agreement to buy the land, the above-mentioned proposal to take a lease having been dropped. Finally, on 1 December 1908, the Deed conveying the land to the Trustees for £3,000 was signed and the transaction was completed.

---

[53] Mr Beale was to retain Belmont Lodge and the back garden of Belair where the squash courts were later to be built
[54] £7,300 in 1908 is equivalent to approximately £650,000 today allowing for inflation - Bank of England statistics

The Trustees gave Mr Beale a first charge over the property to secure the £3,500 being lent by him, and needed to fund the balance of the development costs payable to Mr Beale (ie £3,800) and any other related expenses as they became due. This they did by borrowing £500 secured by a second charge over the property (as envisaged), the lender being Henry Knipe, and by issuing debentures for the balance. These were £25 debentures (subordinated to the first and second charges) which were issued to members who were to receive interest at 4% per annum out of the Club's income. The financing arrangements were varied in 1912, when the Club's debenture holders agreed, at a special meeting, to Mr Beale transferring his (£3,500) Mortgage to the Royal Insurance Company, the Club paying the costs involved. The sum outstanding in respect of the debentures at that time was £2,835, and proxies were received from 24 debenture holders representing £2,000 (ie more than the $^2/_3$rds required). The largest holdings were those of Henry Knipe, John Gordon and J van Raalte[55] (£200 each), and Alfred Simpson and several others (£100 each). The Debentures were paid off over a number of years out of subscriptions and entrance fees, and the Royal's Mortgage was repaid by instalments and finally discharged on 3 July 1942.

Auction bridge

1908 was also the year in which the first code of laws governing the play of auction bridge was established by a joint committee of the Portland Club and the Bath Club. In about 1903 someone had had the idea that all four players (and not just the dealer and his partner) should have the chance to name the trump suit or elect to play without trumps – the issue to be decided in favour of the player willing to propose taking more tricks than his opponents were willing to commit to. Auction bridge was deemed to be a considerable improvement on bridge whist because it introduced competitive bidding. Each player would bid the number of tricks to be made in excess of "the book".[56] The winner of the auction (the "declarer") would play the hand, and (in order to score points) he had to make the contract bid. Provided he did so, his side earned points for the number of tricks won in excess of the "book", whether or not bid. Undoubled tricks played with clubs as trumps scored six points, in diamonds they scored seven, hearts eight, spades nine, and in no trumps ten. Game was made when one side scored 30 points. Thus, if the declarer made 10 tricks in an undoubled spade contract, his side would score 36 points and make game regardless of whether the contract bid in the auction was one, two, three or four spades. A side making 12/13 tricks would also make a small/grand slam regardless of the contract, and a side winning two games also won the rubber. Any contract could be doubled by either of the defenders and redoubled by the declarer's side, doubling and quadrupling the points scored, but no additional redoubling (as in bridge whist) was permitted. Thus, although players could still play for high stakes, if they so wished, gambling ceased to be an essential part of the game. Often the bidding ended quickly and only if both sides had a long suit or two was the auction vigorous.[57] It was soon realised that there was little advantage in doubling for penalties when an opponent opened the bidding with one of a suit; this gave rise to the "take out double". In any event, auction bridge was seen to introduce compelling new features to the game, and as its popularity increased, so that of bridge whist declined.

---

[55] van Raalte in 1909 presented the Club with the clock in an oak case which still stands in the Centenary Room

[56] There being 13 tricks to be won or lost, the first six were traditionally placed in a stack which became known as "the book"

[57] Alan & Dorothy Truscott, *The New York Times Bridge Book*, 2002, p.14

Pioneers of Aviation

The years 1908/1909 were a watershed in the history of aviation - Wilbur and Orville Wright had been developing a powered flying machine in the USA since 1903, and in 1908 the former demonstrated the capabilities of his bi-plane to potential buyers in France. His passenger/co-pilot was Francis Kennedy McClean (1876-1955), the son of the Club's Founder Member, Frank McClean.

Francis had worked for the Government (the Public Works Department) in India for four years and returned to England in 1902. Two years later his father died and he inherited his estate. In 1906 the millionaire sportsman and owner of the New York Herald, Gordon Bennett, inaugurated the famous international gas balloon race (which bears his name) to encourage technical development, and McClean, who was determined to become an aviator, took part in this event in 1908 and 1909.

1909 was the year in which the French aviator, Louis Blériot, flew his monoplane across the English Channel to win the £1,000 prize offered by the Daily Mail for the first successful crossing by a "heavier than air" craft. In the following year Francis McClean obtained flying licence number 21, and bought land at Eastchurch on the Isle of Sheppey for an aerodrome and a private fleet of 16 Wright-designed aeroplanes which Short Brothers built under licence for him. He used his flying skills to test the planes and gave training facilities to the Royal Navy.

He also shared his father's interest in astronomy and led expeditions to Flint Island and Tasmania to observe eclipses of the sun. In 1912 he flew a seaplane up the Thames passing between the upper and lower parts of Tower Bridge and beneath London Bridge – earning cheers from onlookers, but the disapproval of the authorities – perhaps because he clipped Tower Bridge on the return journey and came down on the river. When the War broke out he joined the Royal Naval Air Service and, after service on the Channel Patrol, became the Royal Aero Club's chief instructor at Eastchurch. He later received a commission in the RAF. In 1926 Francis McClean was knighted for his services to aviation.

8

1909

In 1909 King Edward VII granted Tunbridge Wells permission to call itself "Royal".[58] England had become an urban nation. There were motor cars on the streets, but Victorian Bath Chairs, popular in Spas such as Bath and Tunbridge Wells, were still available for hire. They had hinged front covers and a folding hood, and wooden wheels with a rubber rim. Members could ride down from Mount Ephraim to the Club's new building for one and a half pence, but to be pushed back up the hill not surprisingly cost more - two pence! The town's population had doubled since 1872 to about 38,000; more than half the population was female, many of the women were "in service" in the town's comfortable houses, but women's suffrage was still many years away.

Belair Cottage was duly demolished and the new club-house erected by Mr Beale's firm at 40 London Road - a stylish building with three floors and an impressive entrance overlooking the Common. Iron rings (still in place today) were built into the brickwork to enable horses to be tethered to the building. The architect was Cecil Burns (mentioned above), who was starting a practice in Tunbridge Wells, and who was elected to the Club in 1919. He was to become one of the town's leading architects, and his original drawings for the Club remain in the possession of his firm, Burns Guthrie and Partners, in Calverley Park.

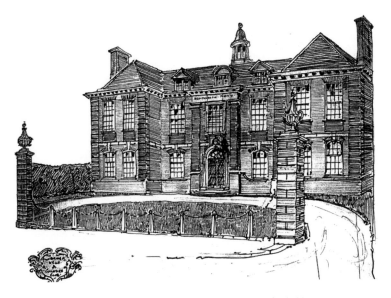

Cecil Burns' sketch of the proposed new Club House
[reproduced by permission of Burns Guthrie and Partners]

On 23 January 1909 the Tunbridge Wells Society newspaper contained the following article which described the proposed club-house and the circumstances which had caused the Club to look for new premises.

---

[58] Chris Jones, *Tunbridge Wells in 1909*, Royal Tunbridge Wells Civic Society, 2008 – this is a fascinating account of everyday life in the year when the town became "Royal"

The Tunbridge Wells and Counties' Club.

For some time past it has been acknowledged that Clubland in Tunbridge Wells has not been what it should be in such a wealthy and aristocratic neighbourhood. The Clubman in the town has perforce had to be satisfied with a makeshift in the form of Rooms at The Great Hall. For over thirty long years he has borne the inconvenience without complaining, until like the proverbial bait for the early bird, he has at last "turned." It is not that he has been oblivious to the inconveniences that the confinement of Rooms afford to those accustomed to regard their Club as their home, *ergo*, their Castle, but the difficulty has been to find suitable premises or land that could either be converted or built upon, and it is only quite recently that the patient Clubman has been able to exclaim, with the ancient Greek philosopher and scientist, "Eureka."

A vacant plot of land, admirably suited for the erection of an extensive building, was discovered in London Road, immediately facing the Common. Successful negotiations followed, and within a short time there will arise therefrom Club premises that will be both a credit to the town and a delight to the members who anticipate finding all Club comforts under its spacious roof.

The old Club will, as far as the members themselves are concerned, remain the same as heretofore, the only difference will be the words "and Counties" added to its title. This was deemed advisable, as there are already County members from Kent and Sussex, and the additional radius that these words imply will doubtless cause many more residents to join from the surrounding neighbourhood, and there is no doubt the town membership will be well increased, in fact we are already assured that many such applications have already been sent in.

It is gratifying to know that satisfactory financial arrangements have been made whereby the entire cost of the freehold site and building, including mortgages relating thereto, will involve absolutely no liability on members.

The entrance fee will be five guineas, and the annual subscription four guineas.

The election of members is vested in the Committee, and, as in the usual way, candidates must be proposed and seconded by members. The ordinary facilities for visitors to become temporary members will exist.

Mr. H. R. Knipe, of Linden Park, is the Chairman of Committee, and Mr. John Gordon, the Hon. Secretary.

Particulars of the New Club.

The building is designed in the English Renaissance style throughout, with red brick facings and rubber brick quoins and tile and slate roof. The segment-arched ground floor windows are divided into oblong panes, and have stone keys which run into a horizontal stone band the whole length of the facade. All windows are cut up into squares, which treatment tends to sooth the inevitable severity of a Renaissance domestic design. The main entrance, which is approached by three stone steps, is a stone projection of simple design, with a semi-circular opening and a continuous architrave, a pair of well-proportioned doors opening under an Adams' fanlight, the whole surmounted by a tablet bearing the Club armorial shield, carved in bold relief, whilst on either side, like impassive sentries, stands a massive brick pilaster on a stone base and brick pedestal, whose caps support a stone entablature, bearing the date, and cornice. This cornice is modillioned and runs the whole length of the building, while again, all harshness is avoided by the three dormer windows which peep shyly over the massive cornice, a softness which is considerably augmented in the projecting wings at either end of the principal elevations and

Suggested Card Room

the central projecting portion, the whole forming a dignified yet charming exterior, and minimises the stand-offish effect which usually accompanies domestic Renaissance treatment. The interior is very spacious, and exceptional accommodation is afforded the members and the staff. The large entrance hall is approached through a tiled porch with porter's box on the left. From the hall rises the main staircase, and direct communication is made between all the principal rooms on the ground floor. On the left is the coffee room, with ample direct servery, and steward's quarters behind, whilst on the right is the reading room ; beyond this is the commodious billiard saloon, adapted for two tables, lighted by a large coved lantern light, also having a perfect ventilation and warming scheme, with a raised dais and massive oak mantle piece.

Under the stairs in the hall is the approach to the excellent lavatory accommodation. All sanitary fittings, both here and elsewhere throughout the building, are by Messrs. Doulton & Co., Lambeth. The scheme throughout is followed on lines of perfect hygiene.

The principal staircase leads to a large upper hall or landing, giving access to a fine card room, a Secretary's and Board room, with adjoining bath room, fitted complete. The chief room of the suite on this floor is the magnificent smoking room, with its coned portion breaking through the actual ceiling and rising considerably above its level. The walls are proposed to be panelled from floor to ceiling of classic design. All the principal doors are either of oak or mahogany, as also are the chimney pieces. A service lift from the kitchen, which is situate on the top floor, runs down to the first and ground floors.

Large cellarage is provided, and a heating chamber in the basement. A telephone box is provided in the entrance hall.

Needless to say the works are being carried out on the most solid lines, and all materials used are of the very best quality.

The size of the various rooms of the Club is as follows :

	Ft.	In.		Ft.	In.
Coffee Room	19	0	by	16	10
Reading Room	28	3	„	23	0
Billiard Room	42	0	„	32	0
Card Room	28	2	„	19	0
Secretary and Committee Room	21	3	„	14	0
Smoking Room	28	0	„	23	0
Hall	28	0	„	20	10

The general colour scheme throughout will be in pale greens and white.

The architect is Mr. Cecil Burns. The builders are Messrs. Beale & Sons, of Tunbridge Wells.

The Opera House.
Hippodrome Season.

A very enjoyable programme is presented this week, at the Opera House ; and good audiences have been the rule at each performance.

A first-class comedian is Albert Hall, who evokes plenty of mirth ; and La Belle Margo shows delightful skill in a pretty trapeze and rope speciality ; a comedy in pictures, entitled " How Ma-in-Law beat the record," causes continuous outbursts of laughter ; a wonderfully clever artiste is Randolph King, who presents his " One Man Programme," and proves to be a veritable host in himself ; Norman Holt, as a raconteur and concertinist creats quite a sensation ; and his principal items fairly bring down the house ; a magnificent picture of the world-renound Italian Calvalry, portraying thrilling manœuvres and sensational military feats is much to be admired ; a dainty comedienne and dancer is seen in the personage of Nina St. Elmo ; The D'arc's wonderful marionettes are in themselves an evening's enjoyment, there are to seen both comediennes and comedians in miniature, all the well known tip-top celebrities of the hall are presented to the admiring gaze of a spell-bound audience, among those who are " At Home " on the miniature stage, are Harry Lauder, George Robey, R.G. Knowles May Henderson, Eugene Fougere, Fanny Field, and others. In the words of the programme, " To describe this act is almost impossible, it can only be compared with witnessing a grand benefit performance and looking through the wrong end of the opera glasses from the grand circle."

Some very realistic scenes of the recent disasterous earthquake at Messina were shown on the screen and were thoroughly appreciated ; this is stated to be the first appearance of these pictures out of London.

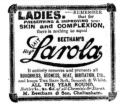

The drawings were made by Robert B Stacy-Judd, who did similar drawings of other fashionable interiors for the same newspaper, and, as they pre-dated the construction of the building, it seems likely that they were prepared for the advance consideration of the members.

Eight months later on or about 20 August 1909 the members of the Club took possession of the new premises which the Courier described in the article below.

THE COURIER, AUGUST 20, 1909.

TUNBRIDGE WELLS CLUB.

NEW PREMISES OPENED.

A PALATIAL BUILDING.

The members of the Tunbridge Wells Club have now taken possession of their handsome new home in London-road, to which the builders are putting the finishing decorative touches. For some weeks the handsome architectural lines of the exterior of the club have been visible; and the favourable impression created by the outside view is confirmed by an inspection of the building, which in its design and construction is one of the finest pieces of work executed in Tunbridge Wells for many years. Mr Cecil Burns, the architect, has followed the Georgian style, and the red brick of the walls, the dignified windows and graceful mouldings combine to give the building a strikingly handsome appearance seen from the roadway. Stately pillars have been erected at the gateway, and the entrance doorway is approached through a piece of ground which it is contemplated to lay out in pretty style. Massive doors of natural oak open into the lobby, and thence the visitor finds himself in the hall, spacious and laid with oak flooring, with a wide fireplace of original design. The first impression of the visitor is that oak enters largely into the general treatment. From the hall, oak doors give admission to the rooms on the ground floor, oak fittings are seen here and there, and a grand oak staircase leads to the first floor. Solid Austrian oak has been employed, every piece of which has been prepared and moulded in Messrs. Beale and Sons' workshops by their own workmen. The natural appearance of the wood has been retained, for beyond a slight waxing the surface has not been specially treated. To the right of the hall is the reading-room, 28 feet by 23 feet in area, lighted by deep windows, and furnished in luxurious style, with comfortable leather-upholstered chairs, the floor covered with a rich Oriental carpet. The billiard room is also on the ground floor, with an outlook to the rear of the premises. It is 42 feet in length, and 32 feet wide, and is a perfectly designed apartment, with ample accommodation for the two tables which have been installed. A raised floor has been constructed around the greater part of the room, and there is a cove ceiling with a top light, twenty feet by ten feet, which is peculiarly constructed, so that while it affords ample light over the tables by day, provides adequate ventilation at all times. Over the tables are suspended six lamp electrical fittings in substantial design. This room, which is fitted in princely manner, is warmed by hot-water radiators, and is also provided with a patent Devon fire-place. The walls are papered in a quiet green tint. Other accommodation on the ground floor consists of a charming little coffee room, porters' and stewards' room, and a perfectly fitted cloak room. All the sanitary arrangements are by Doulton, and the lavatories lined with green and white Dutch tiles. A private telephone box completes the facilities provided for members on this floor. The staircase is five feet wide, constructed of solid oak, with a balustrade heavily moulded and exquisitely worked. A landing is formed at the half-way turn of the staircase, and here a handsome arched window is noticed. The smoking room is the chief apartment on the first floor. From its windows a capital view of the Common is commanded. Twenty-eight feet by twenty-three, it has a special cove ceiling with ventilating apparatus. The chimney piece is in oak, with inlaid panels of ebony and mahogany. On this floor is also the committee room, and the card room, 28 feet by 21; the members' dressing room and bath room. On the top floor are the stewards' quarters, and in the basement the heating chamber and wine cellars. There is a service lift to all floors, with telephonic communication. Electric light is installed through the building, duplicated with gas, and it is heated by means of low pressure hot water.

The new Club undoubtedly forms the largest piece of building work carried out in Tunbridge Wells for some time, and its cost is expected to approach five figures. The substantial character of the work is apparent in every part. Everything used has been of the finest quality, and the members of the Club now feel that they have a worthy home which is a credit to the town and district.

Messrs. Beale and Sons, the builders, have been warmly congratulated on the manner in which the construction has been carried out.

Mr Beale retired in 1910 at the age of 57, and took up travelling to foreign countries and twice around the world.[59] The family business lasted for three generations until 1946, and, as will be seen below, his son was to build the Squash Courts behind the Club.

Club and Post Office, Royal Tunbridge Wells

In 1909 the Club changed its name to the Tunbridge Wells and Counties Club. Adding "Counties" to the name was to encourage more members to join from the surrounding neighborhood. It also reflected the Club's new location close to the boundary between Kent and Sussex, and the fact that new members would be drawn from both counties. Henry Knipe and Alfred Simpson, who had been involved in the development of the new building, steered through the formalities. Knipe was the Counties Club's first Chairman, and Simpson was to succeed him.

48 new members were elected in 1909, compared with only three in the previous year and six in 1907. These included the 4th Marquess Camden, Archdeacon Avison Scott and Sir Walter Murton.

The 4th Marquess Camden

Sir John Charles Pratt, the 4th Marquess Camden (1872-1943) was the son of Sir John Charles Pratt, the 3rd Marquess, and Lady Clementina Augusta Spencer-Churchill. He was educated at Eton and Trinity College, Cambridge, and he married Lady Joan Marion Nevill the daughter of Lord Henry Nevill who joined the Club in 1873. He was a JP for Sussex and Kent, and in 1905 Lord-Lieutenant of Kent. He gained the rank of Major in the West Kent Yeomen Cavalry and

---

[59] John Cunningham, *The Origins of Warwick Park and the Nevill Ground*, Royal Tunbridge Wells Civic Society, 2007, p.43

fought in the First World War. He was decorated with the Territorial Decoration. He was Commodore of the Royal Yacht Squadron in the two years before his death.

Archdeacon Avison T Scott and the Royal Ashdown Forest Golf Club

Archdeacon Avison T Scott (1848-1925) of St James's Vicarage had succeeded Canon Edward Hoare as the town's leading Anglican clergyman. He was a keen sportsman, born on the same day as Dr W G Grace and he had won a cricket "blue" at Cambridge. He was also a golfer (who played at the Royal Liverpool G C, Hoylake) and in 1888, with friends in Forest Row, he had persuaded the Lord of the Manor, Earl de la Warr, that a golf course should be constructed on Ashdown Forest, which was common land. The site had a vital asset, a nearby railway station – the London-Tunbridge Wells train took 1hr 50mins with a 15 minute stop at East Grinstead. Scott used to travel from Tunbridge Wells to Forest Row by train - as if to demonstrate the point that the golf club would attract members from the town. The club they formed was the Ashdown Forest and Tunbridge Wells Golf Club, which was (in 1893) given Queen Victoria's permission to call itself "Royal" and became the Royal Ashdown Forest Golf Club.[60] Scott played golf wearing his distinctive Father Brown hat.

Archdeacon Scott was also ex-officio chaplain of the Workhouse for the aged, infirm and destitute. His sermons were published or reported in the local newspapers and he had a significant influence in the town. He held strong views on Sunday observance, as did other clerics in the Club and the majority of its members.[61] However Scott's approach was tempered by his love of sport. He preached that the English Sunday had played an important part in making England the great and powerful nation it was, but that, although it needed to be a day of rest, it was more important that it was a day of "change", for the week-end party at the country house, the dinner party at the London hotel, the motor-car and the golf links.[62]

Sir Walter Murton

Sir Walter Murton CB (1836-1927) spent his career as Solicitor to the Board of Trade and was knighted for his services to the Government. He was also much involved in local affairs in Chislehurst where he lived and was instrumental in obtaining a Private Act of Parliament to preserve the Common there. He then spent a number of years traveling before moving to Langton in 1907.

Frederick Wadham Elers

In November 1909 Frederick Wadham Elers was elected Mayor of Tunbridge Wells. He had retired as Honorary Secretary of the Club at the end of the previous year after serving in that office since the Club's foundation 36 years earlier. He had done a great deal for the town and the Courier reported:

"Mr Elers has unquestionably earned the distinction by his long and eminent services to the Borough in a variety of ways and he may be expected to grace the civic chair with dignity and business ability in the Council Chamber."[63]

---

[60] Roger Porter, *The Forest Row Golf Club*
[61] See references to the EGM held in 1922 (p.44) and the 1931 AGM (p.48)
[62] Chris Jones, *Tunbridge Wells in 1909*, Royal Tunbridge Wells Civic Society, 2008, p.92
[63] Tunbridge Wells Gazette 28 October 1909

However he found the Council's debates somewhat verbose and unprofitable and, at his Mayoral Banquet, he appealed humorously to his fellow councillors "to reduce the outflow of eloquence". A portrait of Frederick Elers was painted in 1911 by Alexandra Kirk, who specialized in painting local dignitaries at around that time, and was presented to the Club. It hangs in the Centenary Room, and depicts a highly respected gentleman of his time surrounded, as one would expect, by a Deed (doubtless the conveyance of the site of the new club-house) and other papers.

In 1910 the Kent and Sussex Club was founded, possibly succeeding the Nevill Club (which had occupied the Reading Room, the Billiard Room and the Smoking Rooms in the Pump Room)[64] but which had been wound up in 1909. It took over the Tunbridge Wells Club's former premises in the Great Hall, and Alfred Simpson became its President. 20 new members were elected in that year to the Counties Club, and an average of 10 more joined each year between then and the end of 1918. In 1913 Richard Limbery-Buss was elected to the Club's Committee; he served on it almost continuously until his death in 1942.[65]

Frederick Wadham Elers

Bridge in the 1910s

According to the writer Juliet Nicolson, bridge had by 1911 become a passion of the London aristocracy, not only in gentlemen's clubs, and in the new women's clubs, including the Army and Navy in Cork Street and the Empress in Dover Street, to which they were driven in carriages, but also in people's homes.[66] This was auction bridge – but it had a drawback: not enough bidding - the bidding would often remain low because there was no pressure on players to bid to the level of their hands. In 1912 Sir Hugh Clayton (serving the British Government in India) and some of his friends developed a game which included bonuses for bidding a game, and in 1918 the French adopted the same principle in their game of *Plafond*.

[64] J Radford Thomson, *Pelton's Illustrated Guide to Tunbridge Wells*, Pelton, 1883, p.96
[65] Committee Minutes 6 November 1942
[66] Juliet Nicolson, *The Perfect Summer – Dancing into Shadow in 1911*, John Murray, 2006, p.10

9

1914 - 1918

Tunbridge Wells was greatly affected by the First World War. Many young men (volunteers) enlisted and lost their lives. Soldiers were collected in the town from all parts of the country and the wounded were brought from France and other fields of battle to local hospitals. Empty houses became billets, businesses were closed and the streets were darkened at night.[67] The Club remained open, and all officers of His Majesty's Army and Navy were considered as Honorary Members until July 1919 when the Committee decided that that arrangement should cease.

Colonel J F M Winterscale

The Club's Honorary Secretary during the War was Colonel J F M Winterscale who had taken up that office in 1910. He dealt with the mortgages, debentures etc following the purchase of the new building. His efforts during the war years must have been greatly appreciated because he was made an Honorary Member when he retired in 1919. His portrait, also by Alexandra Kirk, hangs in the club-house.

Colonel A T Simpson

Alfred Thomas Simpson, the lawyer, Club Trustee and Committee Member, had risen to the rank of Lieutenant-Colonel in 1906 on assuming command of the 4th Battalion, The Queen's Own (Royal West Kent) Regiment. In 1910 he was transferred to the Reserves with the rank of Colonel and awarded the Volunteer Decoration. When the War broke out, he was 54 but, nonetheless, re-joined and assumed command of the 2nd/4th Battalion. He then organized the Tunbridge Wells Home Guard. In June 1915, he proceeded with his Battalion to Gallipoli and was mentioned in dispatches for his role in the landing in Suvla. Two months later he was wounded and invalided home. By December, however, he was back with his Battalion which had moved to Egypt, and took part in the Senussi campaign where the Battalion distinguished itself. In March 1916 he returned to England and assumed command of the 3rd/4th Battalion. He went again to France in May 1917 and was involved in the Battalion's engagement near Plouvain. In July 1918, having

---

[67] John Cunningham, *400 Years of the Wells*, Royal Tunbridge Wells Civic Society, 2005, p.139-140

been mentioned again in dispatches, he was certified by the Medical Board as permanently unfit for general service and was again transferred to the Reserves.

Michael Panioti Nicolaidi

Michael Panioti Nicolaidi (1863-1920) was elected a member of the Club in 1917. He was a "Levantine", an Ottoman Greek of Italian descent, from Smyrna (now Ismir) in Turkey. He lived with his family at Ambleside, (also called Acropolis), 4 Eden Road, Tunbridge Wells. He knew Charles Hanson who was the Lord Mayor of London in 1917 and attended his Mayoral Ball. He was a merchant and had offices in Smyrna and Fenchurch Street, London. During the War he would have been regarded as an enemy alien, but he worked in Greece for the British Government as an interpreter and also deciphered messages. In view of the German and Turkish naval presence in the Aegean, he wrote personally to Arthur Balfour, the former Prime Minister who had succeeded Winston Churchill as First Lord of the Admiralty, requesting safe passage from the Royal Navy for ships carrying sultanas to Britain. Nicolaidi also obtained a licence (believed to be the only one granted) to trade on behalf of the British Government in large quantities of opium. The opium "runs", which required armed protection, were apparently authorized personally by the Prime Minister, Lloyd George, who was anxious to stop the opium going to America, and to earn significant revenue for the British Government from opium tax. After the war Mr Nicolaidi returned to Smyrna to rescue his business lost to the Germans and the Turks, but he became ill and died shortly afterwards.[68]

Baron Alexander Knoop and the Russian Revolution

1917 was also the year of the Russian Revolution when the last Tsar, Nicholas II, was deposed and all members of the Russian aristocracy were in grave danger. Baron Alexander Knoop and his young wife Olga (born in 1899) were on holiday in Finland (which was under Russian rule) not far from Petrograd (St Petersburg) which was the focus of the Revolution. The Baron's grandfather, Johann Ludwig Knoop (1821-1894) had emigrated from Germany to Russia and founded a textile industry in Narva, Estonia, setting up cotton spinning mills and employing 4,500 people, and building schools and hospitals. In appreciation he was granted the hereditary Russian title of Baron by Tsar Alexander II (1818-1881), which he passed to his sons. Johann's son, and Alexander's father or uncle, was Baron Johann Knoop (1846-1918), a famous collector of violins, violas, and cellos including a number made by Antonio Stradivari, and several of the finest Stradivarius violins bear the Baron Knoop name.

Alexander (surely named after Tsar Alexander II) and Olga fled to England, and arrived in Tunbridge Wells where Baron E Knoop (who was either his father or uncle) was a member of the Counties Club and proposed him for membership. In April 1918 Alexander, who gave the Calverley Hotel as his address, was duly elected to the Club. He found work as an accountant, but in July the members of the Tsar's family, the Romanovs, were murdered and it was a difficult time for Russian refugees.

---

68 Recollections by Mr Nicolaidi's grandson Chas Hill. www.levantine.plus.com

1918 – Henry Robert Knipe

In August 1918, Henry Robert Knipe, the first Chairman of the Tunbridge Wells and Counties Club, died after a long illness. He had given fine service to the town and its institutions including the General Hospital. He had brought "power of mind" not only to Darwin's theories of evolution, but also to the Club's affairs, and had himself provided the equivalent of about £60,000, 10% of the finance required for the new club-house. To show their gratitude, the members commissioned a portrait of him, which was painted by Alexandra Kirk and presented to him. He gave it to the Club and it still hangs in the club-house. When he died the Committee resolved to send his executors a formal tribute to record "*his unflagging interest in the affairs of the Club, his kindly presence which was always welcome and the unfailing courtesy and tact which marked his administration*".

Henry Robert Knipe

In December Colonel Simpson became the Club's new Chairman - his War record commanded great respect, and the members must have been delighted to welcome him into the office which he was to hold for the next 16 years.

- 10 -

THE EARLY 1920s

Cricket at the Nevill Ground

After the War, the Club's members could again look forward to watching cricket at the Nevill Ground - one of the pleasures of the English summer. The 1st Marquess of Abergavenny had made the land for the Nevill Ground available in 1894, and the Tunbridge Wells Cricket, Football and Athletic Club Limited was then formed to conduct the negotiations, acquire a lease and carry out the necessary construction – levelling and laying out the pitches and running track, and building a pavilion and stands. A prospectus was issued to raise the necessary capital. The Marquess was the first President and the original Directors included a number of the Counties Club's members – Lord Henry Nevill, Sir David Salomons Bt, Frederick Wadham Elers, Major Fletcher Lutwidge, Frank Stone and John Stone-Wigg. The Ground was opened in 1898.[69] The wooden pavilion was burned down in 1913 by suffragettes, but it had been replaced.

"WG" had died in 1915, after a stroke *"reputedly brought on by furiously shaking his fist at a German zeppelin flying over his South London garden"*.[70] His friend Lord Harris, Kent's leading cricketer in the 19th century, had become Treasurer of the MCC in 1917, and he succeeded in persuading the House of Lords to declare players' benefit money tax free, as it was an *ex gratia* benefit – to the chagrin of the Treasury.[71] The Kent county team had enjoyed a golden era before the War, winning the County Championship in 1906, 1909, 1910 and 1913.

Frank Woolley (1887-1978) was Kent's star player - a left-handed batsman and slow/medium left arm bowler. He was born in Tonbridge, began his county career in 1906 and made his Test debut for England in 1909. In 1914 (before the War intervened) he scored more than 2,000 runs and took more than 100 wickets.[72] As Neville Cardus wrote: *"To add up the runs made by Woolley - why it is as though you were to add up the crotchets and quavers written by Mozart."*[73]

In June 1920 the Counties Club's Committee, having invited contributions from members, hired a tent on the Nevill Ground for the annual Cricket Week. Kent played local rivals Sussex in a three day match starting on 10 July. Sussex won by six wickets inside two days, but Woolley made 40 runs in Kent's first innings and took four wickets in each of Sussex's innings. The amateurs ("Gentlemen") in both teams were made honorary members of the Counties Club during Cricket Week so that they could use the Club's tent. The Club hired a tent nearly every year until World War II and the Nevill Ground's Committee (of which Colonel Simpson was a member) was permitted to hold its meetings in the Club's ground floor card room.

---

[69] John Cunningham, *The Origins of Warwick Park and the Nevill Ground*, Royal Tunbridge Wells Civic Society, 2007, p.80
[70] John Major, *More than a Game – The Story of Cricket's Early Years*, HarperCollins, 2007, p.348
[71] John Major, *More than a Game – The Story of Cricket's Early Years*, HarperCollins, 2007, p.320
[72] Woolley repeated that feat in 1921/2/3 and scored 1,000 runs in 28 seasons, a feat equaled only by Dr W G Grace. He retired in 1938 with a batting average in first class cricket of 40.75
[73] Neville Cardus, *Good Days*, 1934

Bridge

Playing cards increased in popularity after the War, as families could enjoy their leisure time together. During the 1920s more and more people were learning the game of auction bridge and playing it with their families and friends. One such family was the Pearsons.

John Westall Pearson

John Westall Pearson (1872-1959) was elected to the Counties Club in 1921. He lived at the Manor House in Bishop's Down. His wife, Agnes, bred pedigree bulldogs, and they had two daughters, Matilda ("Maud") (b.1901) and Dorothy (b.1908). John Pearson taught both of his daughters (as teenagers) to play bridge. He was employed by British Oil and Cake Mills Limited and was a Director of the Motherwell Bridge Company Limited (a Scottish steelworks founded in 1898). He also played golf (albeit less well than his younger daughter - see below) and he was the Honorary Secretary of the Tunbridge Wells Golf Club.

At the Counties Club's premises at 40 London Road, one of the upstairs rooms was used for playing cards. In 1922 the elegant Smoking Room became the Card Room, and the Smoking Room was relocated downstairs. An EGM was called at which the members were asked to consider a proposal that the Rule prohibiting the playing of cards on Sundays be rescinded. However, Sunday observance was still regarded as important by the majority and the proposal was rejected by 34 votes to 18. Nonetheless the Committee decided that a second room (the Coffee Room on the ground floor) should be made available for cards, so long as it was not required for any special purpose. This was to be "dependant on the pleasure of the Committee" which suggests that the card-players were to be encouraged, but not given free rein.

Also in 1922 Mr McCausland proposed, and the Committee agreed, that bridge should be played at the Club on Friday evenings, and that a notice be put on the Board to this effect. This minute is the earliest surviving record of bridge being played at the Club.

In 1923 the Committee agreed to limit the stakes for which bridge was played to 2/6d (the equivalent of £5)[74] per hundred points. Richard Limbery-Buse seconded this proposal, and it can be inferred that some members were concerned to prevent the stakes from rising too high. The Committee also decided not to pursue a suggestion that members "cutting in" should be required to play the stakes being played at the table they were joining – saving those who wished to play for less from any embarrassment. The Committee resolved to purchase an up-to-date copy of the Rules of Royal Auction Bridge to keep abreast of changes. Meanwhile whist drives in the town were attracting large numbers of ladies.[75]

In New York in 1923 a larger than life American by the name of Ely Culbertson (1891-1955) married Josephine Dillon, his bridge partner and a teacher at the Knickerbocker Whist Club where he was scratching a living. He had been born in Romania and his mother was Russian. As a

---

[74] This comparison allows for average annual inflation of 4.44% since 1923: Bank of England statistics

[75] The Kent and Sussex Courier of 9 May 1924 reported three whist drives which had taken place that week in the town – one of which at the Pump Room in aid of the Tunbridge Wells and District Nursing Association was attended by 284 entrants (ie 71 tables) and refreshments were served by Girl Guides

student he had become a revolutionary and studied politics and government before finding that he had a particular talent for bridge.

Billiards

Billiards was also a popular game at the Counties Club in the 1920s. There were two full size billiard tables in the club-house's largest room on the ground floor – designed for the purpose. Boys were employed as billiard markers; it was their job to mark and replace balls on the table for the gentlemen players, and to keep the scores. They were required to wear the Club's "livery" and to change and keep their uniforms in the shed behind the club-house. The Committee frequently ordered new liveries for the boys always referred to by their surnames, such as Gates and Kew. They occasionally arrived at the Club five or ten minutes late, and the members were quick to complain to the Honorary Secretary, who had suitable words with the offenders.

The 50 year Jubilee

1922 marked the Club's 50 year Jubilee, and at the AGM Sir John Bromhead Matthews proposed that there should be a reception to mark that event. Ladies were to be invited and the cost was to be met from members' contributions. Unfortunately the proposed reception was cancelled due to insufficient support, but it appears that the Billiard Room was whitewashed and distempered nonetheless.

Lord Richard Nevill

In 1923 Lord Richard Nevill (1862-1939), the 5th son of the 1st Marquess of Abergavenny, was elected to the Club. He was only eight years younger than his brother, Lord Henry Nevill who had joined the Club when it was founded, 50 years earlier. Lord Richard was later to have the honour of escorting Queen Mary around the Pantiles during her visit to Tunbridge Wells.

Lord de L'Isle

Algernon Sidney Lord de L'Isle (1854-1945) the 4th Baron de L'Isle and Dudley of Penshurst Place was also elected. His proposer was his friend Lord Richard Nevill and his seconder was the 4th Marquess Camden, who had joined the Club in 1907 and was married to Lord Richard's niece, Lady Joan Marion Nevill, mentioned above.

Archdeacon Scott

In 1925 Archdeacon Scott died. He had been the town's leading Anglican priest – he had presided over the funeral in the previous year of the Club's last surviving Founder Member, Dr Manser. Scott, who had been elected to the Club in the year when it first occupied its new club-house in London Road, had been a fine sportsman, to whom the members of the Royal Ashdown Forest Golf Club owe special gratitude. The Committee recorded *"that the Club has lost one of its most esteemed members and joined with the community of Tunbridge Wells in mourning the loss of one whose generous sympathies and engaging personality endeared him to the town to which, in the discharge of the duties of his high office, he gave long and faithful service"*.

Also in 1925 James Frederick Dixon, a retired bank manager, became the Club's Honorary Secretary, and was to remain in that important office for the next 31 years.

11

1925 - 1929

CONTRACT BRIDGE

Two booklets entitled *Contract Bridge* were published in the USA in the early 1920s and an application, albeit unsuccessful, was made to the Knickerbocker Whist Club to prepare a code of contract rules.[76]   Somerset Maugham, a serious bridge-player, also referred, in his part-fictionalized memoirs of an espionage agent in the First World War, to a contract version of the game which he had played in Switzerland.[77]

However, the "breakthrough" of contract bridge can be credited to Harold Stirling Vanderbilt, the wealthy American, who led the Americans to victory three times in the America's Cup.   He devised new features and scoring for the game of bridge during a cruise in October 1925 on the *S S* Finlandia, the ship which carried the American team to the 1912 Olympic Games in Stockholm.   Afterwards Vanderbilt wrote the following:-

> "Many years of experience playing games of the whist family were, I think, a necessary prelude to acquiring the background and knowledge needed to evolve the game of Contract Bridge.   Starting as a young boy about 70 years ago, I have played successively over the years: whist bridge, auction bridge and plafond.   I compiled in the autumn of 1925 a scoring table for my new game.   I called it Contract Bridge and incorporated in it, not only the best features of Auction and Plafond, but also a number of new and exciting features; premiums for slams bid and made, vulnerability, and the decimal system of scoring which by increasing both trick and game values and all premiums and penalties was destined to add enormously to the popularity of Contract Bridge.   An ideal opportunity to try out my new game presented itself while I was voyaging shortly after completing my scoring table with three Auction Bridge playing friends on board the steamship *Finlandia* from Los Angeles to Havana via the Panama canal, a nine-day trip.   At first, we were at a loss for a term, other than game in, to describe the status of being subject to higher penalties because of having won a game.   Fortunately for us, a young lady on board the *Finlandia* solved the problem by suggesting the word 'vulnerable'.   We enjoyed playing my new game on board the *Finlandia* so much that, on my return to New York, I gave typed copies of my scoring table to several of my Auction Bridge playing friends.   I made no effort to popularize or publicise Contract Bridge.   Thanks apparently to its excellence, it popularised itself and spread like wildfire." [78]

In short, players would score "below the line" only what they had contracted to make, and overtricks would go "above the line".   Vanderbilt also invented the first bridge "system" which he called "the Club Convention", an artificial opening bid of one club to designate virtually any strong hand.

It is believed that contract bridge was brought to England in 1927 and that Lt Col Walter Buller, a leading player and bridge journalist, was one of those responsible for the game being adopted by the Portland Club.   However there were differences between the ways in which the laws of bridge

---

[76] *British Bridge Almanac*, 2004, p.2
[77] Somerset Maugham, *Ashenden*, 1928
[78] *British Bridge Almanac*, 2004, p.3

were being applied in England and America. The Portland Club addressed the position and in 1927 called a conference of 11 other London clubs to discuss questions which had arisen. In May 1929 the Portland Club invited members of other clubs to attend a conference to discuss contract bridge; points were referred to the Portland's Card Committee which issued a set of provisional laws. In October (in New York) one man who took advantage of the new game was Ely Culbertson, who published the first edition of his magazine *Bridge World*, which soon achieved a circulation of 40,000.

Duplicate bridge

The "duplicate" principle – seeking to remove the element of chance in the deal of the cards – had been tested in whist by Cavendish in London in 1857 and used for competitions and championships in the USA from 1891 as mentioned above. There had also been a duplicate auction bridge tournament (with 30 tables) at an English private house, The Priory in Warwick, which was being occupied by some Americans in 1904. Duplicate auction bridge was played in the USA under the auspices of the American Whist League from 1914. It did not catch on in this country, although it was played informally here: Anne Reese, for example, founded a bridge circle in 1919 which had a fortnightly duplicate auction session.[79] Mrs Reese was a fine teacher and one of her pupils was her son, Terence, who learned to play at the age of seven. However contract bridge was quickly recognised as being more suitable for the duplicate game. The first laws of duplicate contract bridge were established in the USA in 1928; in 1932 the American, English and French laws were co-ordinated into the International Laws of Contract Bridge, enabling international championships to take place and through the 1930s law changes were promulgated by the Portland Club and the Whist Club of New York.

At the Counties Club, meanwhile the main issue, according to the Committee minutes, was the need for more ventilation in the card room. It was agreed that, if four tables were occupied in the Card Room, the Coffee Room could also be utilized for cards. The fire was to be lit in the Coffee Room at 4pm and extinguished at 5.30 if no players were in the room at that hour. There was a quite substantial turn-over of cards - in 1926 the Club received thanks from the General Hospital for the gift of three dozen packs of cards for their whist drives, and in the following year further packs were sent to the hospital for the same purpose. The Club was using cards manufactured in the USA, but the Committee looked into purchasing cheaper cards manufactured in Britain. A decision was deferred until they had obtained samples from John Waddington of Leeds and a quote from De La Rue.

1929 marked the introduction of after-dinner bridge on Thursday evenings. The Honorary Secretary's office was made available for bridge any afternoon and evening, with the exception of the first Friday in the month – when Committee meetings took place. Sir Frederick Dutton wrote to the Committee requesting that the Secretary's office should only be used for bridge if all the tables in the Card Room were being occupied. This situation was apparently a little delicate, for whatever reason, and the Secretary was asked to explain the position to Sir Frederick. The introduction of a Cards Sub-Committee reflected the growing popularity of bridge at the Club.

---

[79] Hubert Phillips article on Anne Reese, BBW August 1935, reprinted in the *British Bridge Almanac*, p.36

12

THE 1930s

At the Counties Club's AGM in 1931 Sir John Bromhead Matthews again proposed that Rule 27 prohibiting the playing of bridge on Sundays be rescinded. Nine years had passed since the members had rejected a similar motion. A great change, he said, had taken place in public sentiment as regards Sundays. He read out correspondence from other clubs which allowed bridge to be played on Sundays; Canon Stone pleaded for the Rule to be allowed to remain, but the proposal was carried by 46 votes to 11.

The membership had fallen from around 180 to 162 and a Special General Meeting was convened to consider the financial situation, it being noted that clubs throughout the world were suffering in this respect. It was agreed to suspend the entrance fee as a means of attracting new members. On display, hanging on the grand staircase, was a collection of stags' heads and antique Japanese swords and muskets, which had been presented to the Club in the previous year by Mrs Hempson; these remained there for some 40 years until they were sold at Christies.

Ely Culbertson

"Bridge" became a household word in the 1930s - first in the USA and then in Britain, largely due to the efforts of Ely Culbertson whom Bertrand Russell called *"the most remarkable, or at any rate the most psychologically interesting, man it has ever been my good fortune to know"*.

In the May 1930 edition of his Bridge World magazine, he offered readers his new *Contract Bridge Blue Book* (for $1.50) and this became a best-seller. In it he developed a scientific approach to the game and promoted the Culbertson system which recognized the importance of the distribution of the cards, and adopted a valuation of honour tricks (as opposed to high card points) and a series of forcing bids, which became the basis of the modern game. Lt Col Walter Buller asserted that a good English team could beat any American team, but Culbertson proved him wrong when he took a team including his wife, Jo, to London and defeated Buller's team by 4,445 points in a 300 board match at the Portland Club. Buller and his team played what was known as "British Bridge" with no forcing bids which it was suggested were *"equivalent to scratching one's head or blowing one's nose to convey information"*. It was generally agreed that the American bidding methods were superior, but noted that the Americans missed a number of game contracts and slams, and that Culbertson did not always follow the rules he had laid down in the *Blue Book*.

Culbertson also faced opposition in the USA from former expert auction bridge players who developed what became known as the Official System, and in December 1931/January 1932 he played his most famous challenge match against a team led by arguably the world's best auction bridge player, Sidney Lenz, who had been Jo's first teacher, who played with Oswald Jacoby. The Culbertson-Lenz match (which Ely's team won) made him a celebrity and he and Jo were summoned to Hollywood to make some films. *"Culbertson had persuaded millions that it was socially unacceptable not to play bridge. ... It was an ideal occupation for married couples during the Depression when there was no television and money was short for restaurants and theatres."*[80]

The Culbertsons took part in further highly publicised bridge matches in England in 1933 and 1934. The first of these was played at Selfridges in Oxford Street, London over six days, and was

[80] Alan and Dorothy Truscott, *The New York Times Bridge Book*, 2002, p.49

watched on a big screen by large crowds and the press from 27 countries, and broadcast daily to the USA, although some of the English newspapers called it "American ballyhoo".

Also in 1931 the original British Bridge League (BBL) was founded as a national administrative body, and local clubs and area associations became affiliated to it. The Gold Cup, the British teams of four championship, the blue ribbon event of the British game, was first played for in 1931, with the final in the following year.

1932 – Scott Page and his bridge league

In 1932 George Scott Page (1899-1988), always known as "Scott" (his mother's maiden name), conceived the idea of starting a bridge league in the Tonbridge - Tunbridge Wells area. As is clear from his autobiography, and confirmed by those in the Club who knew him, Scott was an extrovert and an ebullient character. Still in his teens, he served in France with the Royal Horse Artillery during World War I, and he then played cricket and rugby for Durham. In 1926 he moved to Tunbridge Wells and started his own dental practice. One of his great pleasures was bridge and he discussed with his friends the idea of playing duplicate. There was no club at which that game was played. A knock-out competition was suggested, similar to the Gold Cup which was being reported in the national press, but Scott, being familiar with league cricket, proposed that they should form a bridge league.[81] Amongst Scott's dental patients were John Pearson (described above) and his daughters Maud, who had married Eric Harvey, and Dorothy.

Dorothy Pearson

GOLFERS OF 1931: NO. 34—MISS DOROTHY PEARSON.

Dorothy Pearson (1908-1994) was a fine golfer; having been runner-up in the English Ladies Open Championship in 1927, a member of the English ladies team and the winner of the Kent Ladies Championship in 1928. She played for England in all the home international matches at St Andrews in 1929[82], and won the English Ladies Championship at Westward Ho in 1933.

According to Scott, he "casually" mentioned his idea of forming a bridge league to Maud or Dorothy – possibly when they were in his dentist's chair - probably (he says) not knowing that they were interested in the game. In any event, the fortuitous result was that the Pearsons entered a team in Scott's league. In subsequent years both John Pearson and Maud's husband, Eric, who was a good player, entered teams. John presented the Pearson Trophy and subsequently became Chairman of the Committee running the league. Scott dubbed it *"the second ever duplicate competition after the Gold Cup"*.

[81] G Scott Page, *Recollections of a Provincial Dental Surgeon*, Casdec, 1984, p.128
[82] Picture [left] from the Illustrated Sporting and Dramatic News, 27 February 1932

Dimmie Hill

Phyllis Irene Hill (1911-1996), nicknamed "Dimmie", was Dorothy's best friend from their schooldays, and one of the members of John Pearson's team in the league. Dimmie's father, Stanley, was the headmaster of a boys' preparatory school and her mother was Norwegian. She had learned how to play auction bridge at about the age of nine at her father's school, but only became "hooked" in 1930 when introduced to contract bridge and the Culbertson system whilst recovering in hospital from an appendix operation. In 1934 Dimmie married another league player, Leslie Fleming.

1934 - Acol

In or about 1934, two friends Jack Marx (1907-1991) and Seca Jascha ("Skid") Simon (1904-1948) who was born in Manchuria and educated at Tonbridge School, both relatively unknown bridge-players, began to devise a new system in Acol Road, Hampstead, North London. In 1935 they joined forces to progress their ideas with Maurice Harrison-Gray (1900-1968) who was to become the (playing) captain of the British bridge team, and they were joined by Iain Macleod and later by Terence Reese. Reese and Ben Cohen became Acol's written spokesmen and that system has been widely used in this country since then. Reese and Macleod (both born in 1913) had been on opposing sides in the first varsity bridge match between Oxford and Cambridge (won by Oxford) in 1935. Macleod became a Member of Parliament and, shortly before his untimely death in 1970, Chancellor of the Exchequer.

The originators of Acol recognised the superiority of the Culbertson system, but could also see weaknesses, such as too wide a range for bidding at the one level, and too rigid a system of no trump bidding. They accordingly developed a series of ideas, adopting Culbertson's approach - forcing foundation, a distinctive two bid, and broad principles of natural judgment.

Ely and Jo Culbertson visited Britain again in 1934 and won another USA v Britain match when the home team included the highly accomplished Richard Lederer, and Doris, Lady Rhodes (who is mentioned below). The Culbertsons also visited Cardiff and gave a series of lectures and played exhibition games together. Amongst those present in Cardiff was Basil Tatlow who was one of the early administrators of bridge in Wales who became the Tournament Director of the first Welsh Open Bridge Congress and later (in 1956) President of the Welsh Bridge Union.[83]

Bridge Congresses were beginning to appear on the scene. One such, at the Grand Hotel, Harrogate in 1934, which was due to be attended by 1,500 players, was (according to the Yorkshire Evening Post) banned by the police on the grounds that bridge was a game of chance.[84]

Colonel Simpson

The Tunbridge Wells and Counties Club Chairman, Colonel Alfred Simpson, died in 1934. He had been Chairman for 16 years and on the Committee for 48 years – missing few of its monthly meetings. After the Great War, he had continued in practice as a solicitor and as Registrar of the Tunbridge Wells County Court until two years before his death. He also served as President of the

---

[83] In 1972 Tatlow moved with his family from Llandudno to Tunbridge Wells, as described below
[84] Peter Littlewood, *EBU and County Associations EB 1996*, British Bridge Almanac, p.13. - One assumes that the Congress was to have been for duplicate bridge and wonders whether the decision to ban it was affected by public order or safety considerations

Kent Law Society and Deputy Lieutenant of Kent, and was associated with numerous local associations and sports clubs, including the Royal Thames Yacht Club for most of his life. Colonel Simpson's death marked the end of an era – he had been 13 years old when his father and others had founded the Club in 1872. A large number of mourners attended his funeral, and his obituary in the Courier concluded: "*By his death a gallant soldier and a true gentleman has passed on, but his name will occupy a permanent place in the records of the town and country which he served so well.*"[85]   He was succeeded as Chairman by Frank Weare.

In October Mr Cripps raised the possibility of the Club building a Squash Court behind the club-house to attract new members. It was estimated that this would cost about £2,000 and that 100 new members would be needed to make it pay. Cripps had presumably discussed the matter with Mr Beale, the son of the developer who had built the club-house in 1909, who had retained the land at the rear of the Club, the former grounds of Belair Cottage. However this idea did not commend itself to the Committee.

1935

In 1935 Mr Beale sought the consent of the Committee to build two Squash Courts behind the Club, and this was duly granted – the Club having been given "first refusal". A third of a century later the Club was to acquire the courts – for a brief period.

It was reported to the Committee that the Queen's Own Royal 2nd Battalion of the West Kent Regiment would be marching through Tunbridge Wells on Sunday 16 June and it was resolved to make their officers temporary members of the Club from 2pm that day. Later in the year one of the Committee asked if luncheons could be provided at the Club, but it was pointed out to him that it was impossible to do any cooking on the premises and that extra staff would be required.

1936

The Club's members were playing both auction and contract bridge. The former appears to have remained the "standard" game, because the Committee received a formal request from a group of members to sanction "majority calling" (part of the contract bridge system), and the Committee agreed to permit this.[86]   One member complained that a single rubber of contract bridge had continued for 1hr 45mins and three others (sitting out) had to wait that long to play. It was decided that nothing could be done, but those involved doubtless got the message. It was also agreed that the Club should join the British Bridge League.

Billiards was popular and a handicap competition was introduced for the Bernard Murdoch Challenge Bowl. Richard Limbery-Buse was called upon to organize the handicapping. The billiard markers (now called "page boys") were again in trouble for arriving late and for not paying sufficient attention to the scoring; they received a severe caution from the Honorary Secretary.

The Club's flag flew from the flag-pole, but it was suffering from wear and tear; Major Oliver agreed to replace it. Meanwhile the West Kent Regiment was short of 50 recruits and requested this to be brought to the notice of members who might have employees of military age.

---

[85] Kent and Sussex Courier 7 September 1934

[86] "Majority calling" is today's system where any bid outranks any bid at a lower level regardless of scoring value (*viz* five clubs – 100 points – outranks four spades – 120 points). This superceded "numerical (or value) calling" which was standard in auction bridge in Britain where four spades outranked five clubs because it scored more points

Meanwhile some of the ladies in Scott Page's league were beginning to enjoy national and international successes at the bridge table. Dorothy Pearson played with Dimmie Fleming in the Men v Women match at the British Bridge World Autumn Congress, and in the first session were the top North/South pair. Also, Trixie Lewis played for England against Norway.

1937 - The founding of the West Kent Bridge Club

In 1937 Kathleen Nutting started a private bridge club at her home at 81 London Road, Tunbridge Wells (by coincidence some 100 yards from the Counties Club's premises) to play with her friends. Shortly afterwards, she moved to a larger house at 12 Boyne Park, Mount Ephraim, where she incorporated the West Kent Bridge Club as a limited liability company and became its Managing Director. Scott Page's league was then run under the auspices of the West Kent, and Scott, John Pearson, Dorothy Pearson, Eric and Maud Harvey, and Leslie and Dimmie Fleming became members. Other early members were Trixie Lewis, the Russian Baroness Olga Knoop, Audrey Oswald Smith, Helen Kirk Greene, and Eleanor Young-Hughes.

Dimmie Fleming

Dimmie Fleming also played in London and in Congresses where her talent and potential were spotted. In 1939, shortly before the War broke out, she was selected to play for the British team in the Women's European Team Championship in The Hague. Like most players at that time, she had been brought up on the Culbertson *Blue Book*, and, when she was selected to join the British team, it was on two conditions: that she should switch from Culbertson's bidding system to Acol, and that she should attend training sessions with one of the leading international players, Maurice Harrison-Gray.[87] Acol had proved itself in 1937 when Harrison-Gray, Simon, Marx and Macleod won the Gold Cup. Dimmie's training sessions with Harrison-Gray must have gone well because the British ladies team, including Dimmie, were the Championship runners-up.

Baroness Olga Knoop

Baroness Olga Knoop (1899-1992) was the wife of Baron Alexander Knoop (referred to above); she was tall, slim and elegant. As Richard Cobb wrote in his award-winning book, *Still Life – Sketches from a Tunbridge Wells Childhood*:

"Baroness Olga, the town's only victim of the Russian Revolution, lived in Oblomov-like immobility (not, in fact, prone all day on a sofa, but much of the time seated at the bridge table) in the trough formed by the bottom end of Madeira Park, lending to an area both dowdy and damp and rather run-down the palely reflected prestige of her Imperial Russian title. The Baroness was pointed out to me once, with awe, by Bobby; she had a high fur collar and a bandeau, under a tight-fitting cloche hat, and very long jade earings, and she was smoking a cigarette - in the street, indeed in Lower Madeira Park- held in a long black cigarette-holder, like the advertisement for du Maurier that I used to see in Punch. A sledge pulled by little horses would have completed the tableau; but there was no snow on the red and grey brick pavement which was running with water after a sharp shower. She was the first titled person we had ever seen. What is more, she appeared to be rather beautiful, in a sultry sort of way. The Baroness, like the

---

[87] *Meet Dimmie Fleming*, 1981 Magazine report

"Maudies", seemed to have a horror of heights; but it was quite easy for her to stay entirely on the level, reaching the shops by cutting through Cumberland Walk."[88]

The founding of the Kent County Bridge Association

With the help of his elder daughter Maud, John Pearson founded the Kent County (later changed to "Contract") Bridge Association in 1937. County associations were new, and they were to have a considerable benefit – organizing county competitions and inter-county matches and bringing together talented players from around the county. Pearson had recently retired at the end of a successful career. He had founded and had been Chairman/President of the National and International Associations of Seed-Crushers Associations. For 30 years he had been Chairman and Managing Director of his company, which was taken over by Lever Brothers, and he was a Director of its parent, Unilever. He was a natural leader and he was ready for a new challenge. Maud was the first Honorary Secretary. She and her father built up the county organization from scratch, and she proceeded to run it for some 25 of the next 30 years (ie not including the War years) from the ground floor study of 12 Boyne Park.

The Counties Club

At the Counties Club, meanwhile, the Card Room was getting overcrowded and one of the Committee proposed that the Secretary's Room should also be set out for bridge each evening – preferably for auction bridge. Richard Limbery-Buse asked why this was and the Honorary Secretary told him that he thought that the Card Room was reserved for players of contract bridge. After some discussion it was decided that there was no difference between the two classes of players and matters were to remain as they were.

Limbery-Buse (who had joined the Club in 1899) was living with his wife and their son Geoffrey and daughter Olive at "Florian", a large Victorian house in St John's Road. Geoffrey Limbery-Buse had served as an Officer throughout the Great War and had then worked in films in Hollywood before returning to Tunbridge Wells, and joining the Club in 1933. Father and son were both gentlemen of habit, as described affectionately by their cousin Richard Cobb in *Still Life*:

"Geoff went out every day at 2, carrying a shopping-bag, and dressed, like my father, in an oatmeal jacket and plus-fours. His route was invariable; past the Kent & Sussex Hospital, then along the edge of the Common, past Thackeray's House, a purchase at Romary's biscuit shop, thence to the Tunbridge Wells and Counties Club. As he moved with majestic slowness, he would not reach the club till 2.30. After playing a rubber or two of bridge, he would have tea at the club, then a single sherry; home by the same route, for 6.30. His father left the house at 3.30 after dressing with great care and deliberation between 2 and 3. He did not take Geoff's route, going down to the Five Ways, then down Mount Pleasant and Vale Road, rounding the Post Office, to reach the club, on the stroke of 4, in time for tea. He and Geoff sat at different tables, never played together, and never spoke to one another while at the club. The old man left the club at 6.30, to reach home, by the route on which he had come, by 7. Supper was at

---

[88] Richard Cobb, *Still Life*, Chatto & Windus, 1983. Reprinted by permission of the Random House Group Ltd

7.30 and was the only meal attended by the Limbery-Buse family. Everybody went to bed at 9. .... Old Mr Limbery-Buse represented a link with a Tunbridge Wells that I wanted to be changeless, while knowing that it couldn't be."[89]

Notwithstanding his quaint ways, "Old Mr Limbery-Buse" had served on the Club's Committee since 1913, and also on the House, Billiards and Cards Sub-Committees; he had scarcely missed a main Committee meeting since the end of World War I and his name is mentioned not infrequently in the minutes proposing or seconding motions and thanking others for their efforts.

In 1937 Richard Limbery-Buse proposed that the Club should in future order new cards from the British Legion, and this was agreed. Later in the year one of the members asked if the cards could be changed more often, and the Honorary Secretary said that the contract bridge tables were provided with eight packs per week, and that three gross (ie 432) packs were ordered for the year's requirement at a cost of £27. It was noted that, when the cards at the contract tables were replaced, they were used at the auction tables – evidently the contract players had established "the upper hand". Snooker was a new game being played in the Billiard Room, and it was agreed that there should be a snooker competition.

1938

The Committee was anticipating war. The Honorary Secretary reported that he was in conversation with the town's Gas Officer as to whether the Club could provide a gas-proof room against air-raids which could be used by the public in case of emergency. It was agreed in July that the Coffee and Ground Floor Reading Rooms could accommodate 12/23 people respectively and that the Secretary should write to the Chief Warden to inform him that the Club would co-operate in any scheme for the safety of the citizens of the town.

In the USA Ely Culbertson gave up competition bridge to devote himself to securing world peace.

---

[89] Richard Cobb, *Still Life*, Chatto & Windus, 1983. Reprinted by permission of the Random House Group Ltd

13

1939 - 1945

1939

It was agreed in April 1939 to consult the Borough Surveyor as to the best means of blocking light from the windows in the event of an air raid. After war was declared, the members were anxious to hear the news on the "wireless", but Mr Sherriff Charles, presumably wishing to minimise the disturbance of the bridge players, obtained the Committee's agreement to restrict the volume of sound. New members continued to join the Club during the War, and the temporary rule which applied in World War I, making serving Officers honorary members of the Club, was again introduced.

1940

Tunbridge Wells was in the first line of defence against the risk of a German invasion and men not already in the services between 17-65 years of age were required to register as Local Defence Volunteers. The Battle of Britain was fought nightly in the skies overhead. Day to day living was seriously disrupted, and some 800 bombs were dropped on the town during the War. Numerous properties were damaged, but the town escaped with little loss of life.[90]

The Committee decided that steps were necessary to protect the club-house against fire-bombs: these were to purchase a stirrup pump, two buckets for sand, and a long length of hose, and to ensure that the bath was kept permanently full of water. The basement was made available to the residents of Vale Avenue in the event of air-raids when the Club was closed – after 8pm. In September Richard Limbery-Buse proposed that no teas should be served during air-raids and this was agreed. Members were advised that they would shortly have to find their own matches because the Club's supply was getting low.

The path at the entrance gates to the club-house was rutted and in a bad state due to long frosts, but it was agreed, after discussion with the former Town Surveyor, that, apart from a little rolling, nothing could be done about this.

The gentlemen continued to play their bridge. Table money (6d) remained unchanged, but it was agreed that the card tables should be re-covered. 12 members signed a letter to the Committee stating that they wished to play for higher stakes (namely a flat rate of 6d per 100) - which was agreed. No action was taken in relation to the note in the suggestion book that members should refrain from *post mortems* in the Card Room.

Also in 1940, the English Bridge Union (EBU), which had been formed in 1936, superceded the BBL as the main co-ordinating body, and county associations became directly involved in the administration of the game. However the activities of the KCBA and the West Kent Bridge Club were discontinued until after the War.

---

[90] John Cunningham, *400 Years of the Wells*, Royal Tunbridge Wells Civic Society, 2005, p.143 and 160

1941

In 1941 the Chairman, Frank Weare, died and was succeeded by Neville Stone, the son of Founder Member, Frank William Stone. There were 126 members, 12 were elected, 10 resigned and 4 died. The Ministry of Food acquired the Squash Courts behind the Club to store food.

Staffing became depleted. The Club employed a Steward, Shelford, and his wife and/or sister, one of whom was the housekeeper, and they lived in the self-contained flat on the second floor of the club-house. There was also an Assistant Steward, Shelford's brother, William, and a charwoman and page boys. William Shelford, who had been a driver/mechanic in World War I, was called up to help build tanks, and the charwoman and pages had also left. The Steward, Shelford, also received call-up papers, and the Honorary Secretary wrote to the Rt Hon Ernest Bevin asking if he could be released from military service because the Club was working with a much reduced staff. The Ministry replied that where, as in the case of Shelford, a man is considered suitable for work of national importance, his work could be done by someone older or less physically fit. Shelford's sister came to the rescue by agreeing to work full instead of part-time, but there would be no teas on Sundays and only pots of tea and biscuits on week-days.

Playing-cards and paper were in short supply and it was decided that cards should last for a week. It seems from this that the bridge-players were used to new cards being supplied at least twice a week. They were asked to record scores on "both" sides of the score pads – a small price to pay for the war effort. It was agreed that the Club would be closed for two hours on Christmas Day (from 1.30-3.30pm) so that the Steward could have Christmas lunch with his family.

1942

In March, the Committee agreed at the request of the officer commanding the 22nd Tunbridge Wells Battalion Kent Home Guard that part of the premises should be earmarked as a first-aid post for collecting casualties among the Home Guard in case of enemy action in this country. In June a representative of the Ministry of Health called to discuss the possibility of taking over the Club's premises in the event of invasion, and asked if the Club would (if necessary) allow wire netting to be placed under the glass roof in the Billiard Room and fabric netting in the lower reading room windows and where necessary; this was agreed.

Richard Limbery-Buse chaired the Committee meeting in July 1942. It was reported that Dr Manser from the Kent and Sussex Hospital (doubtless a relative of the Founder Member) had visited the Club and advised that, if an invasion should ensue, the Club's rooms would be able to take in 50 cases. It was also recorded that Royal Insurance had agreed to accept early payment of £500, the final repayment in respect of their mortgage loan made in 1909 to finance the development of the club-house.

The August meeting was to be Mr Limbery-Buse's last and he died in October, aged 81. On his death the Committee minuted: *"Having been a member since 1899 … he will be sadly missed in the Club not only for the services he rendered, but for his popularity. He was persona grata with everyone."*

Also in October, the difficulty of obtaining fuel had become so great that the lights had to go out in the Card Room and the rest of the first floor of the club-house which was closed – but it was agreed that the Lower Reading room would become the Card Room. In December the 22nd Battalion Kent Home Guard advised the Committee that the Club was to become its headquarters in the event of the Home Guard being ordered to man its defences, and requested the use of the premises (with "perhaps" a simple hot meal) for an all-night exercise. Whether such an exercise took place is not known.

1943

In March the Chairman, Neville Stone, died and Dr Trustram Watson succeeded him. It had become even more difficult to buy cards – the British Legion could not supply any and John Waddington could only supply six dozen packs. 18 members petitioned to rescind table money until new cards could be supplied regularly and also to re-open the Card Room on the first floor. They were not to be put off by the War. The Committee responded by informing the petitioners that they would have to be patient for a while – re-opening the Card Room would depend on staff availability, and the number of staff was down to three compared with seven before the War.

Scotch whisky was also in short supply and Chivas Brothers advised that they were compelled to ration supplies to 50% of orders in the 12 months before the War - 13 bottles per month. Six months later supplies of whisky stopped altogether. Gin was still available, although each member was rationed to two singles per day.

1944

The Committee was still considering the possibility of the club-house being bombed, and in April, after discussion with Mr Beale about the likely cost of rebuilding, it was agreed to increase the building's insurance from £10,000 to £16,000.

In July (shortly after D-Day) the Committee saw the light at the end of the tunnel and turned its attention to improving the appearance of the club-house – obtaining estimates for the repainting of the exterior woodwork and rainwater pipes and approving the removal of the posts in the yew hedge at the entrance to the Club. Further signs of better times followed - the Committee authorized the holding of a St Leger Sweepstake.

In November the Committee received from the Portland Club a questionnaire regarding the bridge conventions used at the Club and duly returned this with the Club's response. Unfortunately no copy has been retained.

1945

In September the Committee agreed to sell the Club's "black-out" frames to best advantage. The War was over both in Europe and Japan, so it was agreed to close the Club on Christmas Day. This could not have been done previously, one assumes, without admitting defeat. The result was that the Steward could for the first time spend the whole of Christmas Day with his family.

Part 4   THE POST-WAR YEARS

- 14 -

1946 - 1949

The Counties Club

In 1946 the Counties Club had 117 members. Some had been elected before the First World War - Lawford Andrews in 1885, E R Ashton in 1894, William Charles Cripps (Jnr) in 1899, Douglas Murton-Neale in 1910, Sir Maurice Simpson in 1913 and the Chairman, Dr George Trustram Watson in 1914. It was still a typical gentlemen's social club; bridge and billiards were enjoyed by a number of the members, but not all of them were players.

Two of the long-standing members, Cripps and Murton-Neale, were solicitors, and their law firms, now Cripps Harries Hall LLP and Buss Murton LLP, have been particularly well represented in the Club.

Cripps Harries Hall

William Cripps (1856-1952) had in 1877 joined his father, William Charles Cripps (Snr), in the law firm which the latter had founded in 1852. Cripps (the son) became a powerful force in the local community as a County Councillor, Magistrate and Parliamentary Returning Officer. In 1896 (the year after Sir David Salomons' Motor Show) he defended the first prosecution of a car driver for exceeding the speed limit, then 4mph. The defendant was apprehended by a policeman on a bicycle and accused of driving at twice the legal limit. He was convicted but Cripps must have used his advocacy to good effect because the fine was nominal. Cripps was then instrumental (with John Stone-Wigg) in obtaining the Charter which led to the incorporation of the Borough of Tunbridge Wells in 1889 and in the same year he became the first Town Clerk, which position he held until 1925. At the age of 74 he became a Kent County Councillor and, at 85, an Alderman. He died at the age of 96 and John Cunningham relates that he was President of the St Peter's Rifle Club and that shooting was his "lifelong" hobby.[91]

The two other "name partners" in the firm, Frank Shearme Harries and Geoffrey Sandford Hall, joined the Counties Club in 1919 and 1933 respectively. Frank Harries was head of a four man group of the Council which was responsible for the town's government during the War, and he was later elected Mayor, and an Honorary Freeman of the Borough. Geoffrey Hall, who also joined the partnership in 1933, was proposed and seconded for membership of the Counties Club by his law partners, Cripps and Harries. He had served in the Army during the War and attained the rank of Brigadier, and he was soon to become a Trustee and Chairman of the Club.

Buss Murton

Douglas Murton-Neale was, according to his colleagues, a man of many parts and tireless energy – a founder member of the Nevill Golf Club, a member of Rye and Crowborough and captain of all three. He also had a gun in various shoots. In 1916 he and his law partner, Gordon Bretherton, acquired the firm of Thomas Buss and much later (in 1968) the firm was to merge with Stone Simpson and Hanson to become Buss Stone. The "name" partners of Stone Simpson were Frank

---

[91] John Cunningham, *The Origins of Warwick Park and the Nevill Ground*, Royal Tunbridge Wells Civic Society, 2007, p.41

Stone and his son Neville, and Thomas Fox Simpson and Alfred Simpson, all prominent members of the Counties Club. The other name partner, David Hanson, joined the Club in 1946 and became a Trustee and legal adviser to the Club.

Other long-serving members included John Pearson (elected in 1921), and Charles Preston (elected in 1923), a popular Irishman who had been the Club's Honorary Librarian for many years. James Dixon had been the Club's Honorary Secretary since 1925. These gentlemen were likely to value highly the traditions of the Club.

The West Kent

The West Kent resumed its activities after the War at Mrs Nutting's house at 12 Boyne Park. Mr and Mrs Currie became Managing Directors, but in the next two or three years there were several further changes and eventually the Boyne Park property was sold to Rex Corbett, a bridge-player, who had spent much of the War in Burma.

Dimmie Fleming playing with Captain Parker against Graham Mathieson and Kenneth Konstam. These four (with Terence Reese and Boris Schapiro) made up the team which won the Crockfords Cup in 1950. Mathieson was an outstanding sportsman in tennis, golf and snooker, and a member of Colonel Buller's bridge circus, who won an international tournament in Berlin in 1933; Mathieson spotted Dimmie's talent and coached her. Both he and Konstam were in the winning Gold Cup team in 1949, and Konstam won that cup five times and represented Great Britain regularly until 1965.

In 1946 the West Kent players, Dimmie Fleming, Captain Edward Parker and Baroness Knoop, were in the team which won the Kent County Championship and the Pachabo Cup which in that year became the national championship for teams winning their county events. In 1947 Dimmie Fleming and Dorothy Pearson (playing with Rixi Markus and Doris, Lady Rhodes) won the first post war English Ladies Teams Championship - the Whitelaw Cup. Dimmie Fleming resumed her international career by winning the first post war European Teams event in Deauville, playing with Rixi Markus, Kenneth Konstam and Edward Rayne. Mrs Fleming and Miss Pearson (having won the trials) also played together in the British Ladies Team in the European Championship in Copenhagen in 1948, winning Silver Medals.

Post-war austerity

With rationing in the shops, it continued to be difficult for the Counties Club to buy spirits and fuel for central heating. The Committee was nonetheless able to replace the billiard tables' rubber cushions which were 17 years old and had become very slow. In early 1948, however, the Committee decided that it needed to take urgent steps to improve the Club's financial position. A number of possibilities were considered - opening the Club to members of the Kent and Sussex Club (which was still occupying the Club's former premises in the Great Hall), or affiliating with the Squash Club (whose premises were immediately behind the club-house) or increasing charges for playing billiards and cards, but none of these were found likely to be satisfactory - or providing a bridge-room for ladies.

The admission of ladies to the Counties Club

Brigadier Hall, by then a Trustee, reported that he had ascertained that the West Kent Bridge Club had practically collapsed. He suggested that it might be possible for the West Kent's ladies to be admitted as members of the Counties Club, and it was agreed that he should investigate the position with John Pearson. He then reported back to the Committee that some 60 ladies and 10 gentlemen at the West Kent would like to join the Counties Club. It was proposed that they should all be admitted as members and the Committee agreed that the matter should be put to the members at a Special General Meeting.

That meeting took place on 2 July 1948 and was attended by 47 members (nearly 50% of the total). The Chairman, Dr Trustram Watson, reported on the financial position of the Club and said that the number of members was continuing to fall. Increasing subscriptions would not bring in enough money; charges for the Club's amenities such as cards and billiards were lower than at other clubs, but increasing these would be particularly unpopular; there had been some discussions with the Squash Club but they had proved abortive. The best solution, he suggested, would be an amalgamation with the Tunbridge Wells Bridge Club (evidently the name which the West Kent was then using). He said that he and Mr Hall had met with the Secretary of the Devonshire Club in Eastbourne which had found itself in a similarly difficult situation after the War and had increased its membership significantly by allowing ladies to become members of the bridge section. Mr Hall told the members that it was now the universal practice of London clubs to admit ladies to part of their premises. He said that the ladies were prepared to have their rooms upstairs and to use the side entrance to the Club in Vale Avenue. The minutes then state: "*Mr Pearson, one of the oldest members of the Club and Chairman of the Tunbridge Wells Bridge Club, informed the meeting that in the old days the membership of the West Kent Bridge Club was 90 ladies and 50 men, but owing to the breakaway the number likely to join the Counties Club would be about 60 ladies and 10 men which would yield £250 in subscriptions and card table money of some £400 to £500 besides the income from teas etc. Ladies, he said, don't like coming in by the side door - he thought it rather humiliating*". The matter was put to the vote, and it was agreed that ladies should be permitted to join the Club. It was not, however, agreed that they could use the front door.

At the next Committee Meeting it was agreed to order two gas stoves for the Ladies' Bridge Room and to set up a sub-committee to meet with the ladies to discuss decorations. The Chairman was asked if ladies would be allowed to play in the Men's Bridge Room and he replied in the negative.

Audrey Oswald Smith

Audrey Oswald Smith prided herself on being the first lady member of the Counties Club – from the West Kent. She had founded the Tunbridge Wells Music Club in 1926, and her husband, Harry, was a local doctor and a friend of Scott Page; he had played rugby for Scotland and became President of the Scottish Rugby Union in 1949. Mrs Oswald Smith became one of the Counties Club's original lady Committee members and remained a doyenne of the Club for the next 35 years.

Nancy Starling was another of the original lady Committee members – also married to a doctor, Cyril Widmerpool Starling, who had joined the Club 24 years earlier, and he rejoined. Dr Starling was also a colleague of Scott Page; he had been appointed anaesthetist at the Kent & Sussex Hospital in 1928 and was also the Pearsons' doctor.

Other new members of the Counties Club in 1948 included John Pearson's two daughters (Maud and Dorothy), Dimmie and Leslie Fleming, Scott Page, Helen Kirk Greene and her husband Leslie (an international croquet player), Trixie Lewis, Eleanor Young-Hughes, and Baroness Olga Knoop.

Another lady who joined the Club then was Diana Cobb, the mother of Richard Cobb the author of the award-winning book of reminiscences of his childhood in Tunbridge Wells, *Still Life*.

1949

At the beginning of 1949 the Counties Club had 204 members, 122 men and 82 ladies – it would appear that there were about 22 ladies in addition to those who had joined from the West Kent. However, the ladies were required to use the side door of the Counties Club and the rooms on the first floor which were accessible by a separate staircase. Mrs Oswald Smith used to recount how she was required to use the back door, and when she died in 1985 the Committee recorded that *"she had showed her contempt for this nonsense by brazenly entering by the front door!"*

Amongst the new members was Vera Hodgens who had come to Tunbridge Wells from Ireland with her family after the War, and who lived for a while at 12 Boyne Park. The family included Vera's daughter Ethnie, who some 50 years later was to become Chairman. Vera was a good bridge-player, and in 1952 she won a national event, the Anne Reese Cup, playing with Mary Gibbons.

Pauline Drummond (1885-1962) joined the Committee in 1949. She was an American who had been an actress and dancer who starred on Broadway and then in the West End under her stage name, Pauline Chase. She had become famous playing the title role in Peter Pan some 1,400 times before the First World War. Its author, J M Barrie, was one of her friends, as was Captain Scott of the Antarctic.

At the following AGM John Pearson asked if a waiting room and any more facilities could be provided to make the Club more attractive for the ladies. He suggested that the billiards room should be partitioned to provide an extra room for them, but some of the ladies said that they would prefer to continue to use only the rooms assigned to them on the first floor. The Chairman said that the matter would be given serious consideration by the Committee, but it appears that the majority preferred to retain the *status quo*.

Rex Corbett, meanwhile, was determined to revive the West Kent at 12 Boyne Park. He asked John Pearson's elder daughter, Maud, who was using an office there to run the KCBA, to help him and she agreed. Not surprisingly, in view of the restrictions placed on the ladies at the Counties Club, a number of them preferred to play at the West Kent. Dimmie Fleming was playing in London and elsewhere and resigned from the Counties Club at the end of the year; the Committee recognised her status in the bridge world by awarding her Honorary Membership of the Club.

John Westall Pearson
Chairman of the English Bridge Union, 1950
"The Father of Kent bridge"

15

THE 1950s – THE COUNTIES CLUB

1950

At the AGM in February 1950 John Pearson was elected to the Committee, and he served on it for the next five years. The proposal for further facilities for the ladies was raised again. Mr Pearson suggested building a room on top of the billiards room, but this was considered impracticable, and again the matter was deferred. Three rooms were being used for rubber bridge and the stakes in these were 3d, 6d and 1/- per 100 points. Issues arose from time to time as to whether members arriving during a session should be allowed to "cut in" because some members preferred to continue playing in the same partnerships.

Later that year Audrey Oswald Smith proposed, and it was agreed, that the former Committee Room should be made available for competitive duplicate bridge at week-ends. It was also agreed to set up monthly duplicate bridge tournaments and to arrange a match against the West Kent. Not surprisingly rivalry developed between the clubs, but a number of players were members of both, and this number increased as the years went by.

The English Bridge Union (John Pearson)

Also in 1950 John Pearson was elected Chairman of the English Bridge Union. His bridge administration credentials were impressive - he had been involved in, and become Chairman, of the town's bridge league and he had founded the county's bridge association. Although well into his 70s, he had retained his energy and leadership qualities, and his aim was to make bridge as popular in this country as he knew it was in America. He presided over the annual EBU Congress at the Grand Hotel in Eastbourne and addressed a packed house for the prize-giving at midnight. He said that the Congress just concluded had been the most successful ever held by the EBU, and that the attendance was far in excess of previous events. He added: *"Never has an important Congress witnessed the success of so many comparatively unknown players and the almost total eclipse of so many famous personalities"*.[92]

An eclipse can of course be an event of very short duration and the famous players to whom John Pearson was referring included (it is believed) his daughter Dorothy's best friend Dimmie Fleming, Terence Reese and Boris Schapiro. Those three were in the team which won the Gold Cup in 1950 and they also won the Crockfords Cup together in 1949 and 1950.

Terence Reese and Boris Schapiro

Terence Reese (1913-1996) and Boris Schapiro (1909-2002) formed a remarkable bridge partnership after the War. Together they won the first two Portland Pairs events in 1946 and 1947, four European Team Championships, and one World Team Championship (the Bermuda Bowl) in 1955 – the only British victory. They were also in the winning Gold Cup team together eight times.

Reese, Britain's most famous bridge-player, had learned to play bridge at a very tender age. He was educated at Bradfield and New College, Oxford where he was a classics scholar. He won

[92] *The Contract Bridge Journal*, November 1950, p.29

numerous national and international events during his bridge–playing career, and he wrote a vast number of books that made major contributions to the game, including two, *Reese on Play* and *The Expert Game*, which are recognised by the American Encyclopaedia of Bridge as classics. As a journalist he wrote weekly columns for the Observer from 1948 and daily articles in the London Evening News which merged with the Evening Standard.

Schapiro was born in Riga, Latvia; his family moved to St Petersburg in 1912, and in 1917, they (like the Baron and Baroness Knoop) fled from the Revolution. He learned to play bridge at the age of 10 by watching his father. He was educated at Clifton and Sheffield University, and at the age of 20 he played with Oswald Jacoby in the 1929 Auction Bridge Pairs World Championship in New York. In the following year Jacoby was Lenz's partner in the famous Culbertson-Lenz match mentioned above. Schapiro partnered Jacoby again (this time playing contract bridge) in 1932 when they won the World Pairs Championship. Jacoby is recognised as one of the world's great players, but interestingly: *"Jacoby's weakness in the view of some critics was a penchant for psychic bids, bluffs that were liable to give trouble to partners as well as opponents."*[93] Whether Jacoby psyched when he was playing with Schapiro is not known, but some years later Schapiro was to be troubled "closer to home" by his partner's psyching – as will be seen below.

Schapiro also won the World Mixed Teams of four in 1962, partnering Fritzi Gordon – the other two team members being Nico Gardener and Rixi Markus, and his Gold Cup victories (including eight with Reese) totalled 11, the last one being in 1998 at the remarkable age of 89.

1951

At the Counties Club's AGM in February 1951, it was noted that the accounts didn't make good reading, and agreed that more new members were needed. The separation of the ladies was still an issue and Mr Hallward said that his sister was a member who played bridge, but that he never had a chance to meet her. It was agreed that the men's Reading Room should become a common room where members and their wives could meet after 2pm. However, at a Special General Meeting later in the year some of the traditionalists expressed strong views and the decision at the AGM was overturned.

In the following year Mr Cripps died – he had been a member for 53 years and was regarded as the "Father" of the Club. Dr Trustram Watson resigned as Chairman in the hope that a younger man could take over, but his elected successor was A J Mitchell, one of the Club's Trustees who had joined the Club in 1927. In 1954 Mr Pearson again asked to have the Reading Room opened to ladies at all times, but he was again out-voted. In the following year however, the tide was beginning to turn when it was agreed that there would be a mixed AGM as well as separate AGMs for the ladies and gentlemen.

1955 - *Moonraker*

In 1955 Ian Fleming (1908-1964), a bridge-playing member of the Portland Club, wrote the third of his James Bond adventures, *Moonraker*. This contained a classic scene set in a gentlemen's club when Secret Agent Bond plays a high stakes game of bridge with his superior "M" against Sir Hugo Drax, who is suspected of cheating – unheard of in a gentlemen's club! Bond sees Drax dealing the cards over a reflective cigarette case and proves himself to be an even more talented

[93] Alan and Dorothy Truscott, *The New York Times Bridge Book*, p.45

card-sharp, in the line of duty, by introducing a stacked pack and dealing Drax a hand containing all the honours, (except the Ace and Queen of Clubs and the Queen of Diamonds), but which (to Drax's fury) cannot prevent Bond from making a grand slam (redoubled) in Clubs. Fleming (probably with an eye to the reaction of his fellow club-members at the Portland and other bridge players) was quick to have Bond explain to "M" that the hand he chose was devised by Culbertson as a spoof to assist with the conventions he was teaching.[94]

1956

Brigadier Geoffrey Sandford Hall

Brigadier Geoffrey Hall, who had initiated the admission of ladies to the Club in 1948, became Chairman in 1956. He was to hold that office for the next 11 years and become a Vice-President of the Club in 1973 on completion of 40 years' membership. He also became Chairman of the local tax commissioners, Vice-Chairman of the Tunbridge Wells Group Hospital Management Committee and Founder Chairman of the South of England Agricultural Society. Later, in 1972, he was appointed Deputy Lieutenant for Sussex. According to his son, Christopher Hall, Geoffrey was not a bridge-player but he was asked to take the helm at the Club at a time when it was going through a difficult period of change and a steady hand was required.

James Frederick Dixon

The first major challenge facing the new Chairman was to find an Honorary Secretary to replace James Dixon [right] who died in 1956 after a short illness and 31 years in office. The Committee stood in silence to respect his memory and recorded that he had been greatly loved in the Club, to which he had been devoted and which had become the centre of his life. The Committee had commissioned a portrait of him by a leading artist, Bernard Hailstone, the Government's official wartime artist who lived locally in Hadlow Tower and later became President of the Royal Society of Portrait Painters. The portrait was presented to Mr Dixon who donated it to the Club and it still hangs in the Centenary Room. It captures his character well. James Dixon is in good company because Hailstone's other sitters included Queen Elizabeth the Queen Mother, Sir Winston Churchill and Laurence Olivier wearing his Garrick tie.[95]

Brigadier Hall's proposed candidate was Mrs D M Witt who had been a member of the Committee for three years, but it was unclear whether the Committee would accept a lady as an officer of the Club. However he handled the situation with diplomacy and Mrs Witt was duly elected. She indicated that she would welcome some support in the role, which was also tactful, and Mr T McDowell agreed to act jointly with her. Shortly afterwards, he became the Club's Honorary Treasurer, and Mrs Witt became the sole Honorary Secretary.

---

[94] *Moonraker* is reckoned to be one of the best Bond stories, but its plot was changed substantially to bring it into the "Space Age" when the film was made in 1979, 15 years after Fleming's death

[95] *The Spectator*, 15 December 2007, p.108

1957

The lady members were invited to the Club's AGM for the first time in 1957. They were allowed to use the men's Bar between midday and 2pm and all the other rooms in the Club at any time. They paid three fifths of the men's subscription, but still had no vote at members' meetings. John Lott (b. 1932), whose father Ralph was a member of the Committee, became the Club's first junior member. John, who still enjoys playing rubber bridge at the Club, remembers two schoolmasters playing billiards in the main room on the ground floor - and the lady members purchasing drinks at the stable door between the Bar and the main hall.

1958

In 1958, when the Rules and By-Laws of the Club were re-printed, the lady members (96) outnumbered the gentlemen (76). The former included Pauline Blackwell, the sister of the operatic tenor Peter Pears, who served on the Committee and played bridge most days. On Mondays, in the early days of their membership, the ladies all wore hats, although there is no record of when this practice was discontinued. Evening bridge was discontinued in 1958 owing to lack of support. Mrs Witt gave up her role as Honorary Secretary because she was leaving the district, but the Committee recorded its deep appreciation of the services she had rendered and the great discretion she had shown in attending to the business affairs of the Club. Mrs Crompton was appointed to succeed her. The gentlemen were still keen to recruit more of their number into the Club and it was agreed that members of London clubs, such as Crockfords, the Junior Carlton and the Reform, should be admitted as temporary members without the need for introduction.

1959

John Pearson died in 1959 at the age of 86 - after 38 years membership of the Club. He had been a successful and respected businessman with a great sense of humour and personal charm. In addition to chairing Scott Page's League, founding the KCBA, chairing the West Kent for a spell in its early days and chairing the EBU, he had played a major part in introducing ladies to the Counties Club and serving on its Committee for five years. He was justifiably proud of his daughters, Maud and Dorothy, the latter having represented her country at both golf and bridge. His obituary in Bridge Magazine quoted a line he enjoyed: "*I often forget how many trumps have been played, but I never forget that bridge is a game*". He was modest, but a fine gentleman who can be credited as being "the Father of Kent bridge".

16

THE 1950s – THE WEST KENT

This chapter covers the same period as the previous chapter and so should be read with that in mind.

Rex and Maud Corbett

Rex Corbett married John Pearson's daughter, Maud, and in the early 1950s the West Kent Bridge Club soon recovered at 12 Boyne Park under their joint management. Maud was efficient and popular and she established a friendly atmosphere at the Club and at the events she arranged. Partnership rubber bridge was played on Monday, Wednesday and Friday afternoons and on Friday evenings, when there would typically be five or six tables. Four duplicate competitions took place each month, and trophies were introduced. The Mitchell Cup was presented in 1950 to be awarded to the winner of an annual cumulative post-handicap score event for all comers. This was followed in 1951 by a Pairs Championship, and a Points Cup which was started as an annual cumulative score event. Later, the Kirk-Greene Cup was added – an individual competition for the leading 16 players in the Club playing with a number of different partners over a three month period. The first winner was Amy Price, Bernie Waters' aunt, who used to say, mischievously, "*I always play better by myself!*"

The July 1952 edition of the Contract Bridge Journal contained the following article about the West Kent together with the picture of its premises in Boyne Park which appeared on its front cover.

Also in 1952 Maud's two sons, John and Michael Harvey (b.1929 and 1933 respectively), who were both good players, formed a Junior Section at the West Kent for under 25s. Amongst the Juniors were continuing members Ethnie Hodgens, Ann Hunt and Heather Nettleton (the daughter of John Lushington) who with her husband John joined the West Kent in 1955/56 – John as a beginner. Another was Bernie Waters (b.1929): he played as a Junior with the Harveys and was also a friend of Scott Page at the Tunbridge Wells Tennis Club. Bernie (like others) did National Service and was commissioned into the Queen's Own Royal West Kent Regiment. In 1959 he took leave while serving in the Sudan to play with his sister in the Mixed Doubles at Wimbledon. He also played squash at the Tunbridge Wells Squash Club.

CONTRACT BRIDGE *Journal*

THE OFFICIAL MEDIUM FOR ENGLISH BRIDGE UNION NEWS

THE WEST KENT B.C.

2/6

VOL. 6   JULY, 1952   No. 9

West Kent Club.

by our Travelling Correspondent

Tunbridge Wells is one of the hot beds of Bridge in the country and one of the chief centres in the popular West Kent Club.

The Club was originally founded by Mrs. Kathleen Nutting in 1937, the premises then occupied being at 81 London Road, Tunbridge Wells. In January the Club moved to its present premises at 12 Boyne Park, Tunbridge Wells, and was incorporated as a Limited Company, with Mrs. Nutting as Managing Director. Ten years later Mrs. Nutting resigned and Mr. and Mrs. Currie became Managing Directors. In the next two years there were two or three changes but in October 1949 Mr. R. H. Corbett became proprietor. Shortly afterwards he married the popular and efficient Hon. Secretary of the Kent County Bridge Association, known to all and sundry as " Maud ". Since then the club has gone from strength to strength.

Since its formation in 1937 the Kent C.B.A. have always used the West Kent Club as Headquarters. The very healthy and progressive state of the Association is due in no small measure to its connection with the club and to the continual work put in on it's behalf since its inception by the President, Mr. J. W. Pearson and by Mrs. Maud Corbett.

The Club premises are delightfully situated with three comfortable and well furnished Bridge rooms—as well as two other rooms in the proprietor's private flat which can be made available to accommodate an overflow. A small but well stocked bar is ever ready to minister to the needs of the members whether it be the celebration of victory, the drowning of sorrow or merely the quenching of an honest thirst. Last but not least there is a large car park, which is a great asset and a charming garden, in which for the greater part of the year members may stroll and commune with Nature, enabling them thereby to cool off and forget their own and their partner's errors.

The atmosphere of the Club is one of great friendliness both amongst the members themselves and towards the many visitors who are always welcome. Everything possible is done to ensure that a good time is had by all.

Partnership Bridge has proved very popular and four partnerships are held regularly every week. On Monday and Friday afternoons for a 3d. stake and Wednesday afternoons and Friday evenings for a 6d. stake, Wednesday being one of the most popular days when a 3/- help yourself lunch is provided. This is invariably a case of " House Full ".

For the Duplicate minded there are four regular competitions each month. Aggregate scoring on the 1st Saturday and Match-pointed scoring for the Winter and Summer Cups on the 3rd Saturday in every month. In addition to these regular competitions, Miss Young-Hughes the Club's energetic Match Secretary arranges a series of most enjoyable inter-Club games. Last year

7

CONTRACT BRIDGE JOURNAL - JULY 1952

apart from the regular games with Beckenham, Sidcup, Rochester and Worthing, the Club played against the Ladies Championship Team, which brought back the trophy from Venice ; Oxford University and Crockfords Club. Although, not unnaturally, they were beaten, the Club teams acquitted themselves well and were by no means disgraced. Perhaps the most remarkable recent performance of the Club team was in a heat of the Whitelaw Cup when the side consisting of Miss Young - Hughes, Mrs. Erskine, Mrs. Palmer and Mrs. Oswald Smith defeated a London team consisting of Mrs. Markus, Lady Rhodes, Mrs. Fleming and Miss D. Pearson, by 4 match points after being 28 m.p.s. down with only 10 boards to play (No, the favourite was *not* nobbled).

The Club is proud to claim the membership of three international players, Mrs. A. L. Fleming, Miss Dorothy Pearson and Capt. E. B. Parker, as well as the winners of this years Anne Reese Cup, Mrs. Hodgkens and Mrs. Gibbons also Dr. & Mrs. Hunter the 1952 winners of the London Flitch. The array of National and Congress Trophies on the sideboard has to be seen to be appreciated.

An unusual and amusing situation arose recently in a Pairs event and even now nobody knows the answer.

West secured the contract in two spades. *East* led a heart and *South* put his cards on the table as dummy. Work that one out. What is the penalty ? Do all South's cards become penalty cards ?

The standard of play at the club is of a high standard. In a recent cup match Baroness Knoop a very enthusiastic member found herself in five diamonds as West. After North had opened the bidding originally with one heart and South had responded two hearts, the Baroness (Olga to her friends) now took a chance vulnerable and bid three diamonds. Over North's three hearts, East jumped to five diamonds. Very reasonable.

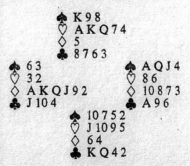

North led ♡ A K and then switched to a club. Up went the Ace and two rounds of trumps was followed by the spade finesse. When it held, Olga immediately saw the possibility of getting home. Four more rounds of trumps leaving ♠A J 4 on table with ♠6 and ♣J 10 in her own hand. The possibility duly materialised—South was helpless. Yes it was a top all right.

By the way, our old friend Percy Chartess has been assisting at the club for the last 12 months and has plenty of scope for producing some of his famous charts.

When next you are in Tunbridge Wells, give the club a visit, you will be very welcome.

8

Maud Corbett at 12 Boyne Park in 1953
with her first corgi

The Juniors would play bridge after work on Fridays, starting at 9pm. John Lott who joined the West Kent in 1953 recalls that, after midnight, they would switch to pontoon and gamble until the early hours. The inevitable noise caused Maud Corbett to fear complaints from the neighbours, or (worse – John says) waking her husband. John Lott also played in a junior team with John and Michael Harvey in the monthly Sunday afternoon Winter League (presumably the successor of Scott Page's league) and in an annual "Age and Impudence" duplicate competition.

As described in the CBJ article above, the West Kent players were distinguishing themselves. Dimmie Fleming and Dorothy Pearson had become celebrated players. In 1950 Dimmie had become the first lady to win the prestigious Gold Cup. In 1951 and 1952 she was a member of the British team which won the European Ladies Championship. In 1953 she became the first woman to play for Britain in a European Open Teams championship in Helsinki, where her partner was Peter Swinnerton–Dyer and her team were the runners-up to France. Also in that year she won the Portland pairs with her husband, Leslie. Dimmie and Dorothy together won the Lady Milne trophy in 1951 and 1953 and the Whitelaw Cup in 1951, 1953 and 1959.[96]

The English Bridge Union (Dimmie Fleming)

In 1955 Dimmie Fleming became Secretary of the EBU. She ran that organization for the next 20 years, first from an office at 9 Frant Road, Tunbridge Wells, and then from two large rooms and a basement store at 12 Frant Road. During that period the EBU's membership grew from 4,000 to 19,000 and Dimmie became "the face" of bridge in England. In 1957 she became a member of the British Bridge League Selection Committee.

The Kent Contract Bridge Association

Maud Corbett continued to run the KCBA as its Honorary Secretary. Its Committee meetings were held at her home, 12 Boyne Park, and Dimmie joined the Committee. In 1958 the Committee decided to hold a Congress, and Maud was deputed to find a suitable venue. Having selected the Grand Hotel in Folkestone, Maud organized the KCBA's first Congress there in 1959.

The event was attended by 261 entrants, most of whom paid an entrance fee of £2, and there was a net profit of £63. It was deemed a success and accordingly became an annual event which Maud organized and hosted each year.

---

96 Peter Hasenson, *British Bridge Almanac*, 77 Publishing, 2004

Maurice Harrison-Gray

Maurice Harrison-Gray (!900-1968), who before the War had been one of the group who developed the Acol System and who helped bring Dimmie Fleming into the national team, visited the West Kent to give a lecture and explained the answers to competition problems he had set (see over). He remained at the head of the game in Britain, winning the Gold Cup (which he had won first in 1937 as described above) again in 1947,1949,1962 and 1966-1968 (a final hat-trick). He was also the bridge correspondent of the London Evening Standard and Country Life.

Baroness Olga Knoop

In the 1950s Baroness Olga Knoop met Dorothy Kerin who, in 1948, had founded Burrswood as a nursing home in Groombridge. The house had been designed by Decimus Burton in the 1830s as a home for Sir David Salomons, the uncle of Sir David Lionel Salomons.

Baroness Olga Knoop [left] with Princess Marina Chavchavadze (of the Georgian royal family)
in the garden at Burrswood in 1953

Olga and her husband Baron Alexander went to live there later when Alexander was suffering badly from Parkinson's disease. He was cared for there and nursed by Olga for several years until he died in 1965. She was after that a regular visitor and travelled all over Europe raising funds for Burrswood, which after Dorothy Kerin's death in 1963 became a charity and continues today as a Christian hospital and place of healing.

WEST KENT CLUB.

BRIDGE COMPETITION

Problems set by M. Harrison-Gray.

In each of the following auctions you are South, your partner North having dealt at game all. System: Approach-Forcing *without* Blackwood or the Culbertson 4—5 No-Trump Convention.

1.

North	East	South	West
No bid	No bid	1 Club	No bid
1 Diamond	Double	?	

What do you bid with the following hand :

S K 9 3
H 6
D A K 10 4
C A Q J 9 5 (6 points)

2.

North	East	South	West
No bid	1 Heart	No bid	No bid
Double	1 Spade	?	

What do you bid with the following hand :

S K 10 7
H Q 9 6 3
D A 6 3 2
C Q 8 (6 points)

3.

North	East	South	West
No bid	No bid	1 Heart	2 Clubs
Double	No bid	?	

What do you bid with the following hand :

S A 10 3 2
H A K 9 6 4 2
D 8
C J 9 (6 points)

4.

North	East	South	West
No bid	No bid	1 No-Trump	2 Hearts
2 Spades	No bid	?	

What do you bid with the following hand :

S K 10 4
H K 9 2
D K Q 10 5
C A J 3 (6 points)

5.

North	East	South	West
No bid	No bid	1 Diamond	No bid
1 Heart	No bid	1 No-Trump	No bid
3 Diamonds	No bid	?	

What do you bid with the following hand :

S A J 9
H 6 2
D A Q 7 4 3
C A 9 4 (6 points)

6.

North	East	South	West
1 Club	No bid	1 Spade	No bid
2 Hearts	No bid	?	

What do you bid with the following hand :

S J 10 7 6 4
H 9 8 5
D A 6
C J 9 3 (6 points)

7.

North	East	South	West
1 Spade	No bid	2 Diamonds	No bid
3 Clubs	No bid	?	

What do you bid with the following hand :

S A 10 5
H 6 4 2
D K J 9 7 3
C K 8 (6 points)

8.

North	East	South	West
1 Spade	No bid	2 Clubs	No bid
3 Clubs	No bid	?	

What do you bid with the following hand :

S 10 9 5
H 10 3
D A K 8
C K J 9 8 2 (6 points)

9.

North	East	South	West
1 Spade	No bid	2 Hearts	No bid
2 Spades	No bid	?	

What do you bid with the following hand :

S J 10 6
H A K 7 6 4 2
D K 9 3
C 10 (6 points)

10.

North	East	South	West
1 Diamond	No bid	1 Heart	No bid
2 Spades	No bid	2 No-Trumps	No bid
4 Hearts	No bid	?	

(a) How many cards in each suit does North hold ?

(b) What do you bid with the following hand :

S 10 8
H Q 10 8 5 2
D K 3
C A 9 8 2 (10 points)

11. At game all, with East the Dealer, the bidding has proceeded :

East	South	West	North
1 Heart	No bid	2 Clubs	No bid
2 Spades	No bid	2 No-Trumps	No bid
4 Hearts	No bid	No bid	No bid

The hands of West (dummy) and South are as follows :

West	South
S 9 6 3	S K J 2
H 8 7 4	H Q J 9
D A 9 7	D K Q 10 2
C K Q J 10	C 8 5 4

South leads the King of Diamonds, dummy plays the 7, North the 5 and East the 4.

What card should South lead at Trick 2, and why? (12 points)

12. The following hand was played in a match-pointed pairs contest, and at several tables the final contract was Six Hearts by West, instead of an easy Six Diamonds by East.

West	East
S —	S Q J 9 5
H K 10 9 8 4	H A 7 3
D 10 8 6 2	D A K Q 7 4 3
C K J 10 7	C —

Against Six Hearts, North leads the 6 of Clubs.

West can try to make this unpromising contract in three different ways, but in at least one of them he may have to count on imperfect defence by the opponents.

Outline these three methods and state which, in your opinion, offers the best chance of success. (24 points)

Answers must be received by the Secretary of the West Kent Club, 12, Boyne Park, Tunbridge Wells, not later than 12th February.

Do not forget to enclose 2/6 entry fee for the Competition and a further 2/6 if you wish to attend the Lecture at the West Kent Club (lecture only 5/-) at which Mr. HARRISON GRAY will explain the answers.

Newman Clark, Printers, Tun Wells.

17

THE 1960s – THE COUNTIES CLUB

1960

In 1960 the Counties' Committee agreed to extend Honorary Membership to the Vale Royal Bridge Club on Tuesdays and Thursdays from 2pm, when a suitable room would be put at their disposal. The Vale was made up primarily (if not solely) of members of the Counties Club who wished to arrange their own private sessions of rubber bridge. The Committee also agreed to replace the gates to the forecourt on the basis that it would not be turned into a car park, which was not then contemplated.[97] In the early 60s the Club experienced a fall in its membership which caused continuing concern to the Committee. In 1964 the ladies were formally welcomed to the AGM and they agreed to discontinue their separate AGMs.

1965 – Duplicate bridge at the Club

Bridge at the Club received a timely boost in January 1965 with the appointment of Capel Guest and his wife Joan as Joint Secretaries. Capel was responsible for bridge and the Bar, and Joan managed the catering and cleaning of the club-house. They were paid a joint annual salary of £780 plus 5% of card table and billiard money. Capel was a keen bridge-player and he re-vitalized the game at the Club and was responsible for introducing regular duplicate sessions on Wednesday afternoons. Capel also introduced a portable roulette table which was popular until the need for a gaming licence caused its use to be discontinued.

In February a new class of evening members was introduced – "duplicate members" entitled to play bridge two nights each week at a reduced annual subscription, but with no vote at General Meetings. Such members could apply for full membership if they so wished, but the Club remained in the "control" of the rubber bridge players, and continued to be perceived by many as a rubber bridge club.

Voting was an issue again in November that year when Harold Cowen wrote to the membership to point out that the lady members contributed most of the Club's revenue and suggest that their non-entitlement to vote was unfair considering that a man joining the Club acquired at once a full proprietary interest. This situation was soon to be rectified.

1966

At the 1966 AGM, the Chairman reported a loss of £406 - subscriptions were (he said) lower than they had been in 1886, but there had been an extremely happy Christmas Party attended by more than 80 members and friends. He thanked Mrs Barnes for her services as Honorary Secretary for the past five years. Richard Warner joined the Counties Club and he was later to become Chairman of the West Kent.

1967

As from 1 January 1967, when Brigadier E P Dangerfield became the new Chairman of the Counties Club, the ladies became full members of the Club on a par with the gentlemen. The Rev H M Piercy became Honorary Secretary; he helped amend the Club's constitution, but had to

---

[97] The forecourt became a car park in 1968

resign for health reasons and his wife took over the role. In that year there was a substantial increase in income from subscriptions, card fees, catering and Bar takings, and much of this success of the Club was attributed to the popularity of Capel and Joan Guest who were made Honorary Members. One of the members, Mrs Crompton, presented the Club with six prints of the *Cries of London* which are hung in the club-house.

1968 – Negotiations with the Kent and Sussex Club

In 1968 Harold Shuter OBE became Chairman. The Club's financial situation was again giving cause for concern and, at the AGM, it was agreed that, in order to increase revenues, negotiations should go ahead with the Kent and Sussex Club with a view to sharing the club-house with them. The KSC, another gentlemen's club, had taken over the Counties' former premises in the Great Hall in 1909, and was expecting to have to vacate those premises. The proposals were to sub-divide the ground floor of the club-house and grant the KSC a lease of the Billiard Room, part of the Reading Room and part of the men's cloakroom. Discussions took place and agreement was reached in principle; planning permission was obtained for the proposed alterations and a draft lease was prepared.

However these efforts were in vain because, as the Chairman reported to the Committee in June, the KSC was able to negotiate an extension of its lease in the Great Hall. The Chairman, looking for alternatives, referred to the possibility of a merger with the Squash Club, but saw little financial advantage in pursuing that course. A more interesting project might be, he said, to approach the West Kent Club to see if their members would be interested in being absorbed into the Counties Club. It was agreed that the Chairman should write to Mrs Corbett (whose husband Rex had died in the previous year) to sound her out.

1969 – Proposal to amalgamate with the West Kent

Mr Shuter reported that Mrs Corbett had replied to his letter and expressed her willingness to discuss the possibility of an amalgamation. This was complicated by the fact that the premises used by the West Kent formed part of Rex Corbett's estate. After discussions, the Counties' Committee (which included Daphne Lee who was later to become the first lady Chairman) came to the view that the best solution would be to incorporate the rest of the membership of the West Kent (ie those who were not already members of both clubs) into the Counties Club. The West Kent had 184 members (10 more than the Counties Club) of whom 140 were believed to be active, and 25 were already members of the Counties, and it was anticipated that about 110 would be willing to transfer to the Counties Club.

The Committee's proposal was considered at a Special General Meeting of the Counties Club's members held on 5 January 1970. Some concerns were expressed about reducing the value of members' shares in the Club and the implications of the 1969 Gaming Act. Trustee and former Chairman, Geoffrey Hall, argued that the increase in membership and activity would guarantee the future financial stability of the Club, but the majority of those present rejected the proposal on a show of hands. Perhaps members were afraid that the atmosphere at the Club would change. Not surprisingly, the Committee took this as a vote of "no confidence" and resigned. Those who offered themselves for re-election were re-elected.

18

THE 1960s – THE WEST KENT

In 1961 Rex and Maud Corbett went to live at the House of Owls, Boar's Head, Crowborough. However they retained the ownership of 12 Boyne Park and continued to use it as the West Kent's club-house. Maud also continued to run the KCBA as its Honorary Secretary until 1968.

Rex's niece, Daphne Gilbert, took over the day to day running of the West Kent for the next two or three years. One of her friends at the Club was Eric Crowhurst who played much of his bridge in London and went on to win all the major bridge tournaments including the Gold Cup. He also wrote numerous books on the Acol system and made an important contribution to bidding theory, giving his name to the Crowhurst convention.

Ray White

Raymond Arthur Cecil White (1930-2004) and his wife Madeleine were amongst the new members attracted to the West Kent. They had previously played bridge with friends at their home in Kemsing where they established a private bridge club. Ray later joined the Counties Club and was Chairman of that club and of the KCBA for many years.

Another new member of the West Kent in the early 60s was John Murrell who joined the under 25s Section. His parents played social bridge and he played at school (necessarily in the cellars because the game was regarded as gambling and against the school rules). He then went up to Queens' College, Cambridge, where he read classics. Chess was his first love, but he also played bridge for the college. He then taught at the Skinners' School. John played in the above-mentioned bridge league for several years, and Scott Page became his principal bridge partner. He also played in a team with Scott, and Capel Guest and "Tiny" (ie 6ft 7ins) Tyrwhitt-Drake (who also played croquet for England) and they competed in the KCBA's Arnold Cup.

The West Kent, aided by Dimmie Fleming's connections, also attracted some of the country's leading players. These included Terence Reese and Boris Schapiro .

England v Northern Ireland at the West Kent

Terence Reese and Boris Schapiro were members of the England team which in the early 1960s played a match against Northern Ireland which the West Kent hosted at 12 Boyne Park. There was an excited audience which included John Lott. The players wore dinner jackets as was the norm. Reese and Schapiro being so well known for their playing skills, their opponents were seen to be underbidding. Reese responded with some "psychic" bids.[98] There was clearly no partnership understanding, which would have made the bids illegal, because Schapiro reacted angrily, and left the table to get himself a drink at the Bar, which was where he remained. To the amusement of the spectators a substitute had to be found to complete the match for England.

1963 - The British Ladies v a Young England team

Reese was also present in July 1963 when the West Kent hosted a remarkable match between the British Ladies team (which was to win the World Olympiad in the following year) and a novice

---

[98] see page 64 above

Young England team. This was reported in the local press [below] which included a comment by Terence Reese that the final match had been one of the best in which he had been involved.

NOVICE BRIDGE TEAM MAKES HISTORY

It defeats international side

BRIDGE history was made in Tunbridge Wells on Sunday when the novice Young England team defeated the British team by three International Match points. On Saturday they had defeated the British ladies by 49 points at the evening session.

The West Kent Bridge Club in Boyne Park was packed with supporters from all over the south east on both days for the sessions which were almost without precedent in the town. Only the Britain v. Northern Ireland match a few years ago attracted comparable players.

One enthusiast said, "It was like having the final of the World Cup played in Tunbridge Wells at the Culverden Stadium."

QUITE A FLUTTER

The young England team was formed several years ago to encourage young people to play the game. This year after the team had been selected the expected international challenge against Young Germany did not materialise and the contest against the British team and the British ladies was specially arranged to take its place.

Mrs "Dimmie" Fleming, the secretary of the English Bridge Union of Frant Road, Tunbridge Wells, who played in the ladies' team and helped to organise the weekend said, "After we lost on Saturday night the British team was mildly amused. On Saturday it was our turn to be amused."

"It will cause quite a flutter in bridge circles."

After the final board on Sunday Mr Terence Reese, one of the world's most famous players, said that the final match had been one of the best he had ever been in. He praised "the exceptionally fine organisation of Mrs Cor-

Special Advertiser feature

THE MEMBERS of the British Ladies team before Saturday's match against Young Britain at the West Kent Bridge Club, Tunbridge Wells. Mrs. "Dimmie" Fleming (standing), the secretary of the English Bridge Union, played in the ladies team. She lives in Frant Road, Tunbridge Wells

The 1964 World Teams Olympiad in New York

Dimmie Fleming was a member of the British teams which won the European Women's Championships in 1959 and 1963 (adding to her previous victories in 1951 and 1952), and the Women's World Team Olympiad in 1964. The other members of the winning Olympiad team were Rixi Markus, Fritzi Gordon, Dorothy Shanahan, Jane Juan and Mary Moss. Terence Reese, Boris Schapiro, Kenneth Konstam and Maurice Harrison-Gray were members of the British Men's team which was 3rd equal in the men's event.

The 1965 World Championships in Buenos Aires

1965 was to be a year of drama. Dimmie Fleming was in Buenos Aires for the World Championships (the Bermuda Bowl) and wrote reports on the play for *Bridge Magazine*. During this event Reese and Schapiro (playing for Britain) were suspended by the World Bridge Federation after their American opponents suspected Reese of making signals to his partner by the way he held his cards – specifically by indicating the number of hearts he held. Reese told the WBF Appeal Committee that he would probably withdraw from international bridge, but this should not be taken as an admission of guilt, and that Committee reported that the British team had sportingly conceded the match with the USA.[99] The editor of *Bridge Magazine*, Ewart Kempson, could not believe that Reese and Schapiro were cheating; he hoped that they would be exonerated on appeal and so did not publish Dimmie's reports. Reese and Schapiro were subsequently found not guilty by a quasi-judicial inquiry, presided over by Sir John Foster QC, MP and General Lord Bourne, held at the behest of the British Bridge League. The Inquiry concluded that there was no sign of cheating in the bidding or play of the cards. Rixi Markus (who was not in Buenos Aires) wrote an article in support of Reese and Schapiro for the American magazine, *Bridge World*. She criticized Ralph Swimer (the non-playing British Captain) for failing in his duties as a captain and not standing up for his team members. He sued her for libel but (most unusually) the jury was unable to reach a decision. Reese wrote a book justifying his actions, and Alan Truscott wrote a book condemning him, and so the situation remained unclear.[100]

Lundie Rees

A bridge-playing contemporary of Reese, but not to be confused with him, was William Ellis Lundie Rees (1911-1993) who assisted Maud Corbett at the West Kent and the KCBA during the 1960s. Lundie was a civil engineer who had been a county golfer and water polo champion, whose sporting career was brought to an end when he was seriously injured by shrapnel during the D-Day landings in Normandy in 1944. He had dabbled at bridge as a boy, and had clearly become adept because, whilst recovering in hospital, he was invited to play in a match for Surrey. After retiring from the Army as a Major in 1950, he moved to Kent with his wife Mary and they ran a village shop in Capel and kept a pig farm. Lundie then devoted himself to bridge which had become a passion. He became a member of the West Kent and one of the stalwarts of the Club. Lundie and Leslie Fleming provided sage advice to youngsters (including Bernie Waters) as to how the game should be played.

Lundie was elected to the Committee of the KCBA in 1961, and in 1965 he became its Honorary Treasurer. He was also Match Secretary and Publicity Officer, but gave up these responsibilities when he was appointed Secretary of Crowborough Golf Club in 1966, but in that year he and Maud did win the KCBA Dyer Smith Cup for mixed pairs.

He also served on the Committee of the Surrey County Bridge Association. In 1966 Surrey's Bridge Congress was in danger of having to be cancelled when the proposed venue became unavailable at very nearly the last moment. Members of the Bridge Committee, including Lundie, looked around for alternative venues. The solution found was one of the first bridge cruises

---

[99] Alan Truscott, *The Great Bridge Scandal*, Master Point Press, 1969

[100] It was reported in 2005 that a friend of Terence Reese had revealed (after all concerned had died) that Reese told him that he <u>did</u> make signals (for the purposes of a book he was writing) but that he and Schapiro deliberately made no use of them – see www.telegraph.co.uk and an article by Andrew Robson in The Times of 5 November 2005

(Vanderbilt excepted), a five day trip from Southampton to Bremerhaven provided by Chandris Cruises at a cost of £25. The bridge was interrupted, however, on 30 July only by England beating Germany in the World Cup Final which was shown live on German TV. The cruise was a great success and Lundie and Mary Rees went on to organise many more cruises in the Mediterranean, Greece, the Baltic and Spain - forerunners of today's bridge cruise industry.

The Kent Contract Bridge Association also held its 1966 Congress on 28-31 July, also on a cruise ship, *QSS Arkadia* - Maud Corbett having had difficulty finding a suitable hotel venue, possibly because hotels were increasing their prices. The cruise price was £28-10s per person, but there were only 56 attendees, well down on the previous years. The Congress returned to the Grand Hotel, Folkestone in the following year, and a few years later it moved to the Leas Cliff Hotel.

In 1967 Rex Corbett died. His widow, Maud, kept the West Kent going at 12 Boyne Park. In the following year she resigned as Honorary Secretary of the KCBA, but she remained Congress Secretary.

In 1969 Mike Griffiths joined the West Kent after being transferred to Tunbridge Wells by his employer, the National Provident Institution. He had graduated with a degree in mathematics from St Catherine's College, Cambridge where he played weekly duplicate bridge at the university club and in various college and university teams. Mike also played for the Kent team and considered that the standard of bridge on Tuesday evenings at the West Kent Club was then as high as could be found anywhere in the county. In 1970 he played in Baroness Knoop's team comprised of West Kent members which won the Arnold Cup.

Notable within the circle at the West Kent at the end of the 1960s/early 70s were the hostess Maud Corbett, Leslie and Dimmie Fleming, Baroness Knoop, Peggy Palmer, Daphne Gilbert, Ray and Madeleine White, Richard Warner, Audrey Oswald Smith, George Scott Page, John Murrell, E (Tiny) Tyrwhitt-Drake, and May Sealy.

- 19 -

THE 1970s - THE COUNTIES CLUB

1970

In 1970 Harold Cowen (who had advocated votes for lady members) was elected Chairman of the Counties Club. Capel and Joan Guest, who had managed the Club for the previous five years, gave notice when Capel became unwell. He returned in the following year to start a bridge school, but that project did not continue for long. Meanwhile Mrs Dredge held herself available to partner any member who for any reason had no partner by 2.30pm on Mondays and Thursdays - the beginning of the "host" system which is common today.

The Committee, anticipating the Club's forthcoming Centenary, arranged for the remaining billiard table to be removed and for the Billiard Room to be completely refurbished for playing bridge and for private functions. The popularity of billiards had decreased over the years and one of the two tables had been sold previously. The work gave rise to a long period of dirt and upheaval, but was completed in time for the Christmas Party when the room was inaugurated as the "Centenary Suite".

In his report at the end of the year the Chairman put a brave face on a difficult financial situation. The Club had made a trading profit in 1970 of £150, but it had a bank overdraft and net current liabilities in excess of £2,000. Something had to be done urgently to increase revenues.

Merger with the Tunbridge Wells Squash Rackets Club

The Committee's previous attempts to secure more income by merging with either the Kent & Sussex or the West Kent Club had proved abortive. In December 1970 the Committee decided to investigate a third possibility previously mooted – an amalgamation with the adjacent Squash Club. The Squash Club was owned by Mrs Dulcinora Picton through her family company. It had been founded in October 1936 when its two courts were opened and exhibition matches were played by A M R Bey (the English open champion), two professionals and one of the founder members, Richard (later Lord) Nugent, who was then ranked the fifth best amateur in the country. Soon afterwards, Alan Picton, who played for Kent, acquired a share of the Club and he later became the sole proprietor through his family company. He devoted much of his time to the Club's affairs (as Honorary Secretary and Treasurer) for the next 23 years until his death in September 1970. During that period the Club became one of the strongest in the country with an impressive fixture list which included matches against the English Ladies team. Alan's daughter, Annette, had played for England at the age of 19 and won the Western Provinces Championship in South Africa, and his son, Clive, was also a good player. When Alan died, the Squash Club lost its main driving force. The Chairman, solicitor Douglas Thomson, was one of its founder members and the senior partner of Thomson Snell and Passmore; a merger with the Counties Club appealed to him as a means of sharing overheads and ensuring the future well-being of the Squash Club. Mrs Picton, for her part, wished to donate money to construct a third court in memory of her late husband.

1971

In early 1971 the Counties Club's Committee decided that that it would be in the Club's best interests to purchase the Squash Club's premises for £15,000 with the help of a £5,000 mortgage.

In August there was a Special General Meeting at which the members of the Counties Club agreed to go ahead – Mrs Picton would grant the Counties Club a 20 year lease of the Squash Club's premises at an annual rent of £750 and an option to purchase the freehold for £15,000, and the rent and option price would increase in line with inflation. The Squash Club's members would all become members of the combined club. The proposed merger with the Squash Club had a most desirable benefit for the Club – which was the agreement of the 5th Marquess of Abergavenny to become President of the merged club.

The 5th Marquess of Abergavenny – the Club's first President

Lt. Col. Sir John Henry Guy Nevill KG, OBE, KStJ, (1914-2000) had succeeded to the titles of his father, the 4th Marquess, on the latter's death in 1954. He was educated at Eton and Trinity College, Cambridge; he fought in the Second World War and was mentioned in dispatches. He was an Honorary Colonel in the Kent and County of London Yeomanry from 1949-61, a County Councillor for East Sussex from 1954-62, a director of Massey-Ferguson from 1955-85, and a director of Lloyds Bank from 1962-85. He was made a Knight of the Garter in 1974 and was Lord-Lieutenant of East Sussex from 1974-89. It was a great honour for the Club to have the Marquess as its first President, coinciding with its Centenary.

The combined club adopted new rules, and the Counties Club reverted to its original name, "The Tunbridge Wells Club". The membership increased to 602, with 365 squash and 237 bridge members. Harold Cowen remained Chairman and Douglas Thomson became Chairman of the Squash Section. A few of the squash players, including Tom Pigott who became a member of the merged Club's Committee and Honorary Treasurer of the Squash Section, Bernie Waters and Sheila Richardson, also played bridge. However the average age of the Counties' members was somewhat higher than that of the squash members and, of course, the activities at the two Clubs were quite different. It was hoped that the Squash members would frequent the Bar at the Counties Club, but they preferred (perhaps not surprisingly) to continue, after showering and changing, to use their own Bar.

1972 - the Club's Centenary

At the AGM in February 1972, the Marquess of Abergavenny took the Chair and expressed his pleasure at renewing his family's connection with the Club. Mrs Picton became Vice-President and Squadron Leader D S Leate AFC, an experienced squash administrator, became Executive Secretary (designate) of the Club. A wine and cheese party followed the AGM enabling those attending to meet the new President. Architects and lawyers were then engaged with a view to obtaining the necessary planning permission to build the proposed new court, but this proved to be a protracted process.

On the bridge side, Scott Page, who had made a major contribution to the game in the 1930s, took over the Chairmanship of the Bridge Committee, and was responsible for the running of bridge at the Club for the next three years. Scott was assisted by Ray White who had been elected to the Counties Club, with his wife, Madeleine, in 1969. Ray was keen to develop bridge at the Club and he persuaded his friends at the West Kent to come and also play at the Counties Club. He was appointed Tournament Director in 1972 and announced immediately that the Club would be happy to welcome KCBA events and to put on other bridge functions.

A special sub-committee headed by Mrs Caroline Thornton organized a party in June 1972 to commemorate the Club's Centenary. The theme was "Tunbridge Wells 1872"; period costumes were worn and the Centenary Room was decorated with blown-up pictures, and toasts were followed by a discotheque.

Geoffrey Sandford Hall

Geoffrey Hall was elected to the office of Vice-President to celebrate his 40 years as a member of the Club. He had played an important part in admitting ladies to the Club in 1948 and served as Chairman from 1956-66 and led the Club through some tricky times.

By August 1972, however, it had become clear that the squash members were dissatisfied with the new arrangements because they could not see any benefits from the merger. Solicitor, Robert Seeckts, who had become Honorary Secretary of the Squash Section, recommended to Harold Cowen and Douglas Thomson that the two Clubs should de-merge and go their separate ways. It was agreed that a sub-committee representing both sections of the Club should review the merger and make recommendations. At its first meeting in September the Squash Section's representatives made it clear that they wished to secede.

Geoffrey Sandford Hall – c 1972

Cowen and Thomson found themselves in a difficult position. They had worked hard to bring about the merger and the former was well aware that the Club desperately needed the extra revenue from the Squash members' subscriptions and court fees. They contended therefore that the new arrangements should be given more time to succeed. A number of meetings were held over the ensuing weeks, but the situation remained unresolved.

John Lushington

Amongst the new members elected in the Centenary year were Percy "John" Lushington (1899-1995) and his wife, Phyllis. John was the grandson of James Law Lushington, who had become a member in 1891. John had played for many years at the London Bridge Club, at Crockfords, and at EBU events, often with his wife as his partner. He had taught all his children, including Heather Nettleton (who had joined the West Kent) to play the game. John and Phyllis lived in North London and he was Managing Director of his family company of wholesale chemists, Sangers Limited. When he retired in 1970, Heather suggested that they should come to live in Tunbridge Wells to be near to the other members of his family. His reply was "*If the Bridge Club's alright, I'll come!*"

1973

In February 1973 Harold Cowen introduced an outline proposal by Hillier Parker to redevelop the Club's premises to take advantage of the merger with the Squash Club, and at the AGM shortly afterwards it was agreed by the membership that that proposal should be given further consideration.

Following the AGM Daphne Lee was elected Chairman, the first lady to hold that office. Her husband was Ronnie Lee who was the Secretary of the Nevill Golf Club. Diana Hill became joint Honorary Secretary of the Club with Robert Seeckts of the Squash Section.

In April it was reported that, if planning permission was obtained, the club-house would be valued at around £135,000. However the Borough Council then "listed" the club-house which ruled out the possibility of it being developed. In June the Club's combined Committee, having considered the situation carefully, resolved that squash should cease to be played at the Club which meant that there would have to be a de-merger, and the Trustees were asked to consider how this should be achieved. Draft Heads of Agreement for the proposed secession were prepared, but the matter took another 12 months to resolve because the financial and legal arrangements needed to be un-scrambled. The situation was complicated by the fact that the Club had incurred significant professional fees and its option to purchase the freehold of the Squash Club's premises was considered to have acquired some value.

Meanwhile, bridge activities were increasing. Ray White used the Centenary Room to give a demonstration of the first bidding boxes (now an everyday sight in duplicate bridge clubs) which were manufactured in Sweden. Ray also succeeded in bringing in new members who also played at the West Kent. One of these was Mike Griffiths, who was asked by Ray to take over directing the Wednesday evening duplicate sessions. Mike was soon to become the Club's Tournament Director.

Brian Lippard, who had moved to Tunbridge Wells in 1971 and was a colleague of Mike Griffiths at the National Provident Institution, was invited by Mike to come and play at the Club on Wednesday evenings. Brian had started playing bridge at school, and continued at Peterhouse College, Cambridge, where he read natural sciences and coxed the College VIII. He met Mike when they were both working in London and playing bridge in the Insurance League, and he too became a member of the Counties Club at the end of 1973.

Over the next two-three years a number of other good players (including Gerald Soper, John Glubb, Bernie Waters, and Peter Quinton) joined in and the standard of the duplicate bridge sessions at the Club on Wednesday evenings began to approach that of the West Kent.

The Centenary Cup was introduced in 1973 as the Club Championship for mixed pairs, and the first winners were Bridget Oettinger and a new member of the Club, Major Basil Tatlow, who had acquired 12 Boyne Park, the West Kent's premises.

At its meeting in April 1973 the Committee discussed an approach by a representative of the West Kent to amalgamate and agreed that this would be pursued further. The new Chairman, Daphne Lee, then wrote to the West Kent with some proposals, but (as described below) these were rejected.

At the end of the year there were 276 bridge members and 321 squash members. Subscriptions had increased from £986 in 1970 to £3,185, income (table money etc) from bridge had doubled to £2,106, and income from squash was £1,099. However there had also been legal expenses and architects' and surveyors' fees of £1,363. The net profit for the year of £701 was not large, but it was an improvement on the previous year.

1974

In 1974 Mrs Blackwell, Lady Brennan and Mrs Langridge were made Honorary Members. The last mentioned was the widow of Walter Langridge who is honoured by a brass plaque in the Bar recording his 50 years of membership (from 1918-1968) and service to the Club, both as a Trustee and as the surveyor advising on property matters.

The termination of the merger with the Squash Club

In June there was a Special General Meeting at which it was agreed that the amalgamation between the Club and the Squash Club had not been the success hoped for and that the secession proposed 12 months earlier should take effect. The Club assigned its lease of the squash courts to the Squash Club, but with an option to re-purchase the premises should they cease to be used for playing squash. The Squash Club paid £1,000 in partial reimbursement of expenses incurred and the Club changed its name back to "The Tunbridge Wells and Counties Club". The Marquess of Abergavenny confirmed that he would be happy to continue as President of the Club.

In July, handicap duplicate bridge was commenced on Monday evenings and proved successful largely due to the efforts of its promotors, "Dai" Dymant and John Lushington. Later in the year Mr Lushington wrote a letter to the Committee, counter-signed by 14 members, suggesting that the partnership (rubber) bridge on Monday and Thursday afternoons should be played in both rooms on the first floor, instead of in the Centenary Room downstairs and one room upstairs. They presumably felt that this would be more cohesive and friendly, but the Committee (in their wisdom) denied the request.

Diana Hill was the Honorary Secretary for the next four years, and she served on the Committee until 1987. She was renowned for her smooth running of the Club and for her excellent catering arrangements. Her husband, David, was a keen golfer, but Diana loved throwing parties. The every-day atmosphere at the Club was buzzing – the Bar would remain open after afternoon bridge until 7pm and members would stay after playing and enjoy spirited conversation. The Annual Report confirmed that the Entertainment Committee had organized three enjoyable parties, and that the new venture of wine and cheese lunches had proved very popular.

However the Club's financial position had been weakened by the loss of the squash members and the professional fees which had been incurred. Diana Hill wrote to all members advising that the Club could not afford to continue paying interest at the current rate of 15% on the Club's overdraft of £4,000, and that there would be a surcharge of 25% on subscriptions until the overdraft was repaid.

1975

The Reading Room on the ground floor became a Bridge Room, at the suggestion (this time successful) of John Lushington who had become a member of the Committee. This room was later named the "Diana Hill Room" in Diana's honour.

The cup and prize-winners included a number of the players mentioned above - the Centenary Cup: Peggy Palmer and Bernie Waters; the Dapple Salver: Mrs Tyrwhitt-Drake; the Flitch Cup: John and Phyllis Lushington; Knock-out Bridge: John Glubb and Bernie Waters; Mixed Pairs: Peggy Palmer and Bernie Waters; Points Cup: Mike Griffiths; and the Process Knock-out: Peggy

Palmer and Scott Page. Mike Griffiths played in the Gold Cup that year with Ray White, Ross Garratt and Brian Lippard, and later with John Murrell, Gerald Soper and Jeremy Willans.

In July the Chairman wrote to his opposite number at the West Kent, Richard Warner, to say that, although the older members still preferred playing rubber bridge, the Club had an increasing number of younger members who were playing duplicate. He suggested that the West Kent should take over the running of the duplicate sessions and proposed that the West Kent's name should be put on the front of the building. Some discussions took place, but the West Kent's Committee preferred to leave matters as they were, and to continue playing at the Masonic Hall.

1976

In 1976 Christopher Hall, the son of the Brigadier who had died in the previous year, became a Trustee. He had succeeded his father as senior partner of Cripps Harries Hall and joined the Club in 1971. Finance was an issue again notwithstanding the receipt of two anonymous donations of £1,000, and the Committee found it necessary to make a special appeal for money. This raised £3,245 of donations and interest-free loans from members. More income was needed and an invitation was sent to the West Kent to make use of the Centenary Room on Tuesday and Friday evenings on a rental basis. However, nothing came of this.

The Abergavenny Cup (honouring the Club's President) was presented as the Club Pairs Championship and the winners for the first two years were Miss D Chipperfield and Anne Mills. The Tatlow & White Rose Bowl was won by Baroness Olga Knoop, Peter Quinton and Mr and Mrs Handley; the Centenary Cup was won by Olga Knoop, Peter Quinton, Scott Page and John Murrell. In May it was agreed to run a duplicate teams event on Saturday evenings.

In December 1976 the Squash Club opened its new court, "the Picton Court" which had been built next to the two existing courts with the funds donated by Dulcinora Picton, and a ceremony was attended by 60 of its members.

1977 - The Club's first Summer Congress

In 1977 Ronnie Halfhead became Chairman of the Counties Club and there was a continuing need for more income. The antique Japanese weapons which had hung on the walls of the main staircase for many years were sold at Christies, raising £1,407.

Ray White and his wife Madeleine organized the Club's first Bridge Congress which took place over a week-end in August. It was well attended by members and their guests including West Kent players. Bidding boxes were used, trophies were presented, and meals were provided. This was a red-letter day for the Club which showed how well its premises could be used for a major bridge event. Not surprisingly, it was agreed that the event should be repeated and in the following year the Committee agreed to invite Maud Corbett, Dimmie Fleming and Richard Warner from the West Kent as guests. The Congress then became a regular annual event under the control of Ray and Madeleine White.

1978

At the 1978 AGM the members considered a motion to change the Club's name to "The Tunbridge Wells Bridge Club". Leslie Fleming cited the fact that none of Crockfords, of which he had been member, the Hamilton and the Portland specified "Bridge" in their names, and Daphne Lee said that she took pride in the Club's foundation in 1872 and gauged that the general feeling of members was that tradition was all important. John Lushington felt that new members might be attracted if the Club's title included the word "Bridge", but the motion was defeated. The Flitch Cup was presented to Syd and Clare Shaw, and the Tatlow & White Rose Bowl was won by Mike Griffiths, Brian Lippard, Gerald Soper and Richard Welch. The Rubber Bridge Knock-out was won by Peggy Palmer and Scott Page.

Also in 1978 Peter Quinton and Baroness Olga Knoop won the Abergavenny Cup. They played regularly together at the Counties Club on Monday and Wednesday evenings and in numerous competitions over many years, including events in Spain, Cyprus and France.

Peter recalls a televised occasion in Paris, when one of their opponents was the film actor Omar Sharif, famous for his roles in the films, *Lawrence of Arabia* and *Dr Zhivago*. When they approached Sharif's table, he got to his feet and bowed deeply to the Baroness. Olga had played in the Gold Cup and Sharif would have recognized her from the bridge circuit, but it is not known how much he knew of her background in Russia. She, however, would have been more than aware of his role in *Dr Zhivago*, the film made in 1965 of Boris Pasternak's novel. That book, banned in Russia, depicted life in Russia at the time of the 1917 Revolution from which Baroness Olga and her husband Baron Alexander escaped, but which must have had a considerable effect on their lives. Lara (played by Julie Christie in the film) was Olga's contemporary. Olga must have enjoyed that moment. However she and Peter were there to play serious bridge. Peter remembers making an unlikely contract against Sharif in Three No Trumps, when he and his partner held between them only 22 high card points and he wrongly identified his (French) Jack as a King.

20

THE 1970s - THE WEST KENT

Vida Bingham joined the West Kent in 1968, and a year or two later she met Dimmie Fleming, not as a result of bridge, but prompted by a totally different activity. Vida, having a lifelong interest in horses, was a frequent visitor to Plumpton, her local race course. One afternoon, when she was paying more attention to the horses than where she was going, she rather forcefully collided with a fellow race-goer. Whilst the latter was regaining her composure, Vida recognised that it was Dimmie and rather hoped that Dimmie wouldn't recognize her. However, this was not to be. So, after mutual apologies, Vida said she was a member and invited Dimmie, who was not, to have a coffee with her in the members' enclosure. Dimmie declined but, when Vida mentioned that there was home-made chocolate cake, she changed her mind.

Both Vida and Dimmie lived between Plumpton and Tunbridge Wells with Vida being nearer to the racecourse. It wasn't long before Dimmie gave lifts to Vida when they went to the races and vice versa to the bridge club. Tea was often enjoyed at one of their houses. After a few months, Dimmie asked Vida to partner her at the West Kent. Vida immediately said "No". Dimmie was taken aback by this rebuff and said that this was the first time anyone had declined to partner her. Vida replied that she didn't feel she was good enough. A little later, after a day at the races, Dimmie stopped off at Vida's house for tea. Vida left Dimmie in the sitting room whilst she departed to the kitchen. On her return, Dimmie announced that she had a confession to make. She was very sorry but she had looked through Vida's handbag, found her diary and booked bridge for the pair of them for the next Tuesday evening. Later that week, tea was enjoyed at Dimmie's house. Leslie asked Dimmie how their bridge session had gone. "Awful" came the immediate reply from Dimmie. *"But she was nervous, so I've asked her again"*. So began a long and successful partnership.

In May 1970 Maud Corbett received an illustrated presentation card bearing the names of 90 members of the West Kent in token of their appreciation of all she had done for the Club over the previous 21 years. This had been beautifully inscribed by one of the members, Mrs Harding-Edgar, who was a book-seller.

Rex Corbett's executors decided, not surprisingly, that 12 Boyne Park should be sold. Maud wished to find a purchaser who would take over the running of the West Kent at the property. That must have sounded like a tall order, but she succeeded when one of Welsh bridge's leading figures, Major Basil Tatlow, and his family, agreed to buy the property, and moved to Tunbridge Wells.

Major Basil Tatlow

Basil Tatlow (b.1897) was a retired accountant who had served during the War in the Pay Corps, but bridge was his passion. He had been one of the hosts when Ely Culbertson visited Cardiff before the War, he had been Chief Recorder at the European Bridge Championships in 1950, President of the Welsh Bridge Union in 1956, and one of the Welsh delegates on the Council of the British Bridge League. He had played three times for Wales in the Camrose Cup (home internationals) and in 1961 he won the Welsh National Pairs and was Tournament Director at the

European Championships.[101] He ran his own bridge stationery business in Llandudno, and his wife Mabel made the card wallets for duplicate bridge. The Major still had WBU commitments which required his presence from time to time, but it was proposed that he would run the West Kent and that his son-in-law, Derick Lewis (who had been working in publishing in Canada), would run the family stationery business.

After purchasing 12 Boyne Park the Tatlows took over the running of the West Kent at the premises. Douglas and Betty Millson joined the Club at that time. Betty had brought up five children and she and Douglas decided that the time had come for them to learn to play bridge. Douglas had in the early 1960s enjoyed listening to Lundie Rees talking about bridge at the Alders, the pub next door to Lundie's village shop. The Major welcomed the Millsons into the Club and visited them at their home at Melrose in Upper Cumberland Walk to give them private bridge lessons. Maud Corbett also invited them to weekly group teaching sessions at her home. Douglas found himself playing in a Tuesday evening session at the Club with Peggy Palmer and some other formidably good opponents, and was most relieved to escape without being heavily criticised.

The Major then asked Ray and Madeleine White to help him run the stationery business, and Mr Lewis, who did not have the same bridge background as his father-in-law, took control of the bridge. Soon afterwards, and against the wishes of the Major, the West Kent was given notice to quit 12 Boyne Park on 1 May 1972 – no doubt for sound financial reasons. It would, after all, have been difficult to operate the club at a profit because of the competition provided by the nearby Counties Club. The house was then converted into flats which were sold.

Maud Corbett was determined to keep the West Kent alive. First she took a room in the Mount Ephraim Hotel for the bridge sessions. Then, a few months later, Douglas Millson, who was a Freemason, arranged for the Club to rent a room in the Masonic Hall in St John's Road at the favorable rate of £5 per session. Maud issued the following calendar [over], showing that in the next month, October, there were to be no less than 12 sessions.

The West Kent could no longer offer the catering and other permanent facilities which had been available in Boyne Park, private parties were not possible, and the membership fell to 53. However there was a Bar at the Masonic Hall and members were trusted to pour their own drinks and to leave the correct money. The Club's Rules were changed; annual subscriptions were reduced from £5 15s 6d (for full members) to £1 and the Club dropped the word "Bridge" from its name. However the continuing members were loyal and keen to play, and there was an average of nine tables on Tuesday evenings, and six tables plus a table for learners on Fridays.

The Maud Corbett Cup was awarded for Winter Pairs and the Rex Corbett Cup for Mixed Pairs. Swiss Teams parties were held on some Saturday evenings and Pearson Cup matches for teams of four took place on Sundays. Maud meanwhile continued with her work for the Kent Contract Bridge Association at her home at the House of the Owls, and for about a year Committee meetings were held there.

---

[101] These recollections about Major Tatlow have been provided by his good friend, Mrs Jessie Newton, who founded one of the first bridge clubs in North Wales (the Garden Village Club, Wrexham) in 1948 and who was herself President of the WBU in 1974

WEST KENT CLUB

Calendar 21st. September - 30th December 1972

SEPTEMBER

Thursday	21st	Practice Class
Friday	22nd	Handicap Duplicate
Tuesday	26th	Duplicate
Friday	29th	Handicap Duplicate AND Practice Class

OCTOBER

Tuesday	3rd	Duplicate
Thursday	5th	KIRK-GREENE CUP FINAL & MENZIES CUP 4th heat
Friday	6th	Handicap Duplicate and Practice Class
MONDAY	9th	Tuesday Duplicate
Friday	13th	Handicap Duplicate and Practice Class
Tuesday	17th	Duplicate
Friday	20th	Handicap Duplicate and Practice Class
SUNDAY	22nd	Kent Pairs Final (Laralry Cup)
Tuesday	24th	Duplicate
THURSDAY	26th	DYER-SMITH QUAL. HEAT (Kent Mixed Pairs)
Friday	27th	Handicap Duplicate and Practice Class
Tuesday	31st	Duplicate

MASONIC HALL NOT AVAILABLE ON TUESDAY 10th OCTOBER.

NOVEMBER

Friday	3rd	Handicap Duplicate & MENZIES CUP (5th Heat)
SUNDAY	5th	DYER-SMITH CUP FINAL (Kent)
Tuesday	7th	Duplicate
Tuesday	14th	Duplicate
Thursday	16th	Handicap Duplicate & Practice Class
SUNDAY	19th	DAILY TELEGRAPH CUP KENT QUAL. HEAT.
Thursday	23rd	Handicap Duplicate & Parctice Class.
SUNDAY	26th	Tuesday Duplicate 2.30p.m.

AS THE HALL IS NOT AVAILABLE there will be NO Tuesday Duplicate in the week commencing Sunday 19th, and the Tuesday Duplicate which should be played on the 28th is arranged for Sunday afternoon 26th instead.
There will be NO Handicap Duplicate or Practice Class on the 9th or 10th.

DECEMBER

FRIDAY	1st	Handicap Duplicate & Menzies Cup (6th Heat)
SUNDAY	3rd	Pearson Cup
Tuesday	5th	Duplicate
Friday	8th.	Handicap Duplicate & Practice Class
Tuesday	12th	Duplicate
Thursday	14th	Handicap Duplicate & Practice Class
SUNDAY	17th	Pearson Cup
		Duplicate

Dimmie Fleming continued to enjoy successes away from the Club. She won the Whitelaw Cup again in 1970 and 1972. Also in 1972 she was elected Vice-President of the English Bridge Union, having been its Secretary since 1955, and became Secretary of its Law and Ethics Committee. She also gave a rare interview to the Jersey Evening Post [right].

1973

Richard Warner

In 1973 Vic Drew, who had been made Chairman of the West Kent, retired because he was leaving the district. Richard Warner [right] was elected Chairman and served the West Kent Club as Chairman for the next 15 years. He was a well-known actor who appeared frequently in leading roles on the West End stage in shows such as Agatha Christie's *The Mousetrap* and *No Sex Please, We're British*. Members of the Club went up to London to see him on stage. He was a good bridge-player and he gave lessons in Sevenoaks where he lived.

Ray White became a member of the West Kent Committee in 1973 and started directing the regular bridge sessions and week-end events.

Dimmie Fleming, bridge champion

BETTY BROOKE found two ladies outside her cottage at Rozel admiring her Clematis montana. She found that they were here for the Jersey bridge tournament and that one of them was Mrs. Dimmie Fleming, ex - world bridge champion, one of the most celebrated women players and the secretary of the English Bridge Union. She spoke about how she had started playing competition bridge and what the game means to a dedicated player.

"I began playing bridge in hospital in 1932 when I was recovering from an appendix operation. The Sister said that a man in the next room had come back from the United States full of enthusiasm for a new game which he had learned over there and would I like to learn to play. I had played auction bridge at school, but the new game of contract bridge was strange to me, and as we both had time on our hands we played together. My friend Dorothy Pearson, who was English lady's golf champion, and Mrs. Hill, the other patient's wife, made a four.

"My first game of contract bridge was, in fact, played on my bed in hospital and I was fascinated by it. I later visited Mr. and Mrs. Hill at their home in Bristol and we had a week-end of bridge together, and I was absorbed by it."

Were there conventions in those early days?

"No—not really. We had Ely Culbertson's Blue Book, and he told us never to bid unless we had 13 points and a five-card suit. In those days before the war most bridge players followed Culbertson.

"I met my husband through bridge, actually. His mother was a bridge player and was in the Tonbridge Bridge League which we formed. I was married in 1934, and although my husband was better known as a cricketer he also plays bridge and indeed we won The Flitch in London. Yes, it's a competition for married couples which is held in London for London and the Home Counties.

"I would not like you to think I did nothing else but play bridge. I was a stockbroker before my marriage and continued to practise until September 3, 1939, when Hitler put an end to that. I have a daughter and two grand-daughters — the younger one was born last month — and I love all sorts of sports. Bridge is very much an occupation for me because as secretary of the English Bridge Union I am kept extremely busy. It's a paid appointment and my job is organizing bridge tournaments.

"In 1939 I was chosen for Great Britain, and we were second in the European Championship. In those days there were few players and I've seen it grow to the popular game which contract bridge is today. It's taken me all over the world. I've played in the States, South America and most of the European countries. During the war there was no bridge but by 1947 the competitions began

again and except for five years I suppose I've played in all the English championships and in 1964 I became World Champion in New York."

How do women compare with men?

"Well, I have to admit that women are not as good on the whole. They lack concentration. I suppose. The finest players I have ever seen are the two Italian champions. Renito Garazzo and Giorgio Belladonna, of the Italian Blue Team are really magnificent players. They are quite outstanding and the Blue Team has won the World Championship 11 consecutive times. Any team which can win 11 times in succession is a very good team.

"What advice would I give an average player ?" Bridge players are divided into competition players and social bridge players. I still like to play rubber bridge socially if I go out to dinner, but of course one improves one's game by comparison and in competition bridge you discover just what other players do with the same hands. This is invaluable. However, I think one can play too much bridge and not enjoy it after a bit. I play only about once a fortnight because I am kept fairly busy with my job as secretary and with other outside interests."

Jersey Evening Post
3 May 1973

David Reich, who had joined the West Kent in 1967, was also elected to the Committee in 1973 and served on it for the next 14 years. He assisted Ray and soon took over as Chief Tournament Director and directed sessions on Tuesday and Friday evenings. New members would play on Fridays and be invited to join the Tuesday sessions when they had demonstrated their capability by amassing 200 or more EBU local points. Elise Williams became Assistant Secretary to Maud Corbett, and she also gave a number of years' service to the Club, and Capel Guest (previously employed by the Counties Club) became Treasurer, briefly.

The West Kent's Committee considered the possibility of an amalgamation with the Counties Club, and there were some talks with Daphne Lee, its new Chairman, who had been a proponent of such a merger in 1969. At the AGM in May 1973 the membership discussed a letter from Mrs Lee in that respect, but rejected the idea of a merger. In the following month the Club requested the Masonic Hall to put its tenancy on a permanent basis with a yearly lease of the room used on Tuesday and Friday evenings.

1974

In 1974 Maud Corbett retired as Honorary Secretary of the West Kent Club, and was elected Life President in recognition of her services. Rex Corbett's niece, Daphne Gilbert, also received a presentation in appreciation of her work for the Club over many years.

Richard and Molly Burrows

Also in that year Major Richard Burrows became Treasurer and his wife, Molly, became the Honorary Secretary. The two of them then ran the West Kent together until 1999 - a remarkable period of 26 years. They dealt from their home at Malt House, Kemsing, with all membership, book-keeping and organizational details. They also promoted the Club and its activities, and ensured that it retained the spirit and ethos instilled by the Corbetts.

Richard and Molly Burrows

Molly was assisted by Betty Millson who became Assistant Secretary and Betty's husband, Douglas, also assisted with the administration of the Club, and Committee meetings were held for many years at their home in Upper Cumberland Walk.

1975

In early 1975, the West Kent had grown again to 121 members. The Committee considered a letter from the Counties' Chairman inviting their members to make use of the Centenary Room at 40 London Road for their bridge sessions, but decided that that would not be in the Club's best interests. David Reich arranged for the supply of some handsome coffee spoons as prizes with an enamel medallion and a red diamond and the Club's name inscribed.

Also in 1975 Jeremy Willans (b.1959), still at school, became a member of the West Kent. He is the grandson of Lundie Rees, who taught him to play bridge. Lundie and Jeremy's grandmother, Mary, had moved from Kent to Langport in Somerset where they ran a bridge club together, and Jeremy would visit them and find his grandfather a most willing teacher and playing partner. They were runners-up in an EBU competition for relatives playing together, and 10th in the following year – not surprisingly the only grandfather/grandson combination.

1976

In August 1976 an informal meeting took place between members of the West Kent and the Counties - Richard Warner, Richard and Molly Burrows, Ray White, Freda Richard and David Reich represented the former, and Messrs Recaldin, Glubb, Lushington and Pengelly represented the latter. No concrete proposals were made, but the Counties' representatives suggested that the West Kent should formulate conditions under which they would be prepared to make use of the Counties' premises at 40 London Road. The West Kent's Committee agreed to make members aware of the position and suggested that they should familiarise themselves with the Counties' club-house on two dates proposed. However, the Club's members remained anxious to preserve the Club's separate identity and it was agreed in December that these discussions should be terminated.

1977

In May 1977 there was a successful Dinner Dance at the Spa Hotel attended by 72 members and friends. In October the Committee agreed that the Chairman, Richard Warner, should write to the new Counties' Chairman, Ronnie Halfhead, regarding the possibility of using their premises. In 1977 and again in the following year the West Kent won the Fleming Femina event. Also in 1977 Ray White became Chairman of the Kent Contract Bridge Association, having been elected to its Committee in the previous year; he was to hold that office until 1989.

1978

In January 1978 Richard Warner reached an amicable agreement with Ronald Halfhead for the West Kent to use the Counties' premises whenever the Masonic Hall was not available, and this arrangement commenced on an *ad hoc* basis.

1979

Mike Kingsland also won the Swiss Pairs at the 1979 EBU Summer Congress in Brighton, playing with Jeremy Willans (aged 20). Jeremy also won the Rothmans Regional Final that year, playing with David Woods. Competitions were frequently sponsored by cigarette manufacturers, and Jeremy's prize included a few hundred cigarettes. Smoking at the Club's sessions was to become an issue in the years ahead. Brian Lippard, who had been a member of the Counties Club since 1973, switched to the West Kent in 1979 to play in the Tuesday evening sessions. In his early days, playing against one of the top players, he was pleased to make a rather difficult contract. This prompted his opponent to remark with something of an expression of surprise "*Oh, he can play then!*" Brian decided to treat this as a compliment although he wasn't entirely convinced.

Mike Kingsland took over from Peggy Palmer as the most consistent regular player at the West Kent during the latter part of the 1970s. He won the Points Cup (for the individual who had scored the most points in the Club's Tuesday and Friday evening sessions) in 1974, 75, and 77-79.

21

THE 1980s

1980

In March 1980 the West Kent Club received notice to quit the Masonic Hall at the end of May. The Committee had to decide between looking for new premises, seeking a merger or sharing arrangement with the Counties Club, or closing the Club.

In April, Richard Warner met with Ronnie Halfhead, and agreed proposed terms on which the West Kent could make use of the Counties' club-house at 40 London Road on a regular basis. These were confirmed in a letter dated 6 May and approved by both Clubs' Committees. The West Kent was granted the right to use the Centenary Room, the two Bridge Rooms on the first floor and all the Club's facilities - on Tuesday and Friday evenings, and at other times by arrangement with the Counties Club's Honorary Secretary. The West Kent would pay a block subscription of £5 per month on the assumption that 140 of their members would play each week, and table money of 25p per head per session. It was agreed that the West Kent would raise its subscription to £2 per head and that its members would become Associated Members of the Counties Club. This was, in a sense, a *de facto* merger, but the West Kent and the Counties Club retained their separate identities and management.

The Counties Club then had 144 full members, 111 associate members and 240 others in a special category, which included the members of the West Kent and of the Vale Club. Receiving extra income from the West Kent and the Vale helped the Counties Club make a welcome profit in 1980 of £3,125.

Those who wished to play duplicate at the club-house on Tuesday and/or Friday evenings could apply to join the West Kent and those who wished to play duplicate at any other time, and/or to play rubber bridge, could join the Counties. The full members of the Counties (who shared the ownership of the Club's assets and could vote at General Meetings) were (historically) those who played rubber bridge and others who paid the full subscription. Rubber bridge still attracted around eight tables at a typical partnership session, although duplicate was becoming more popular, particularly amongst the younger members. Nonetheless, the Counties Club continued to be perceived as a traditional rubber bridge club.

The atmosphere in the club-house was agreeably sociable – members who had been playing afternoon rubber bridge on the first floor would come down to the Bar and enjoy lively repartee, pink gin and whisky – and some (including Peggy Palmer and Daphne Gilbert) would then join in the duplicate, in a very competitive spirit.

Also in 1980 the West Kent members, Dimmie Fleming and Vida Bingham, won the Whitelaw Cup and represented England in the Lady Milne Trophy. Rixi Markus was the captain of the England team. Well into the match, Dimmie and Vida returned to score up after what they felt was a good set of results. One of the hands on which they gained had involved making a six club contract via a squeeze. Alan Truscott was sufficiently impressed with the play of the hand that he subsequently wrote it up in an article for the New York Times. Rixi said nothing about the set, and so Dimmie, looking to boost Vida's confidence, ventured the comment that Vida had played the six club contract rather well. This prompted the response "six clubs is cold". Nothing further was said, and the players went off to play the next set of boards. Dimmie and Vida repeated their success in the Whitelaw Cup and represented England again in the Lady Milne in the following year. Vida has gone on to enjoy many subsequent successes at the bridge table, mostly in team events, winning events in Jersey, Croydon and Tenby, and at the Isle of Man Congress and an international event in Portugal.

When Dimmie Fleming's husband, Leslie, died in 1980, their bridge stationery business was just ticking over. Vida's husband Tom urged Dimmie to continue the business and the revival came from Vida who designed the moulds for the well-known plastic Fleming Boards which replaced the pockets, leather wallets and the earlier wooden boards used for duplicate bridge. Dimmie and Vida ran the business together until 1987 when it was sold.

1981

The Counties Club v the West Kent in the final of the Corbett Cup

In 1981 the final of the Corbett Cup, the Kent inter-club teams event, was contested between the Counties Club and the West Kent. The match was played in the two Bridge Rooms on the first floor of the club-house with a Vu-graph projection for spectators in the Centenary Room. The teams are shown in the photograph below - from left Len Handley, Ray Darby, Dimmie Fleming, Mike Kingsland, Colin Wilson, Vida Bingham, and Bernie Waters (who represented the West Kent) and Anne Mills, Bill Adams, Gerald Soper, Mike Griffiths (front), Jeremy Willans, John Murrell, Brian Lippard (front) and Richard Welch (who represented the Counties Club).

Not pictured but also members of the West Kent team were Diana Avis and Terry Goldsmith. These were all strong players and the match was keenly contested. The Counties team won the match and the Cup, but the West Kent shared the honours because most, if not all, of the Counties' team were also members of the West Kent.

Colin Wilson (b.1949) has enjoyed many successes at bridge since the 1980s. After leaving school, he was employed by British Steel for three years before taking an honours degree in Metallurgy at Leeds University. From 1974 he worked for the Ministry of Defence and lived in Tunbridge Wells. He was introduced to both the West Kent and the Counties Clubs, and his partners included such "luminaries" as John Glubb and Daphne Gilbert. He was elected to the West Kent Committee in the late 1970s and went on to become the Club's Chief Tournament Director. His regular partner in his early days was Freda Richard and they won a number of club events together and also the Pairs Championship at the Kent Congress in Folkestone. Freda was a great character who later emigrated to Australia – she had a cockney accent and (according to Jeremy Willans) enjoyed playing the fruit machine after and during matches. Colin won the West Kent Points Cup (for the aggregate points scored on Tuesday and Friday evening sessions) four times in the 1980s. He and Mike Kingsland both won that trophy 17 times in the period from 1974-2007, and so, during these 34 years, there were no other winners. Fortunately there were other trophies for the rest of the members to play for.

Also in 1981 the KCBA nominated Jeremy Willans as a promising young player for the EBU's Coaching Scheme. Ray White, who joined the Counties Club's main Committee in 1981, continued to run the Club's annual Summer Congress.

On Sunday 2 August 1981, the last day of the Congress, Ray White and Mike Griffiths interrupted proceedings by announcing the news that England had beaten Australia in the 4th Test at Edgbaston by 29 runs. At the start of the day Australia were 9 for 1 in their second innings with a target of 151 to win, but Ian Botham took five wickets for one run in a spell of 28 balls, finishing with 5 for 11. Not surprisingly there were cheers all round. That Congress was adjudged by the Committee to have been a great success and it was recorded that credit was due in particular to Diana Hill.

One of the Committee members on that occasion was Mrs Mona Ives who had been a member of the Committee for 14 years and kept the Club's books. Mona, who had played cricket for England, would have relished the occasion – and recalled the feats of Frank Woolley who had died in 1978 at the age of 91.

1982

In 1982 the West Kent won the Corbett Cup, defeating Farnborough Bridge Club in the final which was again played at 40 London Road. Mike Kingsland, Colin Wilson, Jeremy Willans and Terry Goldsmith won the Arnold Cup.

Bridge teaching was popular in the early 1980s. Maud Corbett continued to give bridge lessons at her home in Crowborough, and amongst her grateful pupils from the West Kent were Brian Ping, Lene Gook, James Johnston and Kevin Rigby.

Angela Tompson was another of Maud's pupils. She joined the West Kent and sat at one end of the room and played with help from Maud and Elise Williams. One evening the duplicate session was short of a pair and she nervously joined in a "real" session. She was then encouraged in particular by the Chairman, Richard Warner, and Richard and Molly Burrows, to play in competitions and take her game to a higher level. She has won a number of county events, including the Kent Mixed Pairs in Folkestone with Charles Snape.

Angela has also been a member of the Counties Club since the mid 1980s, and has taught duplicate bridge to many at the Club since then. She started by teaching a small group of eight, including Yvonne Bowman, but over the years her teaching has grown into nine classes each week with 260 students. One of her pupils was Christopher Hall, Trustee of the Club, senior partner of Cripps Harries Hall and son of former Chairman Geoffrey Hall. Angela has written a book *Bridge with Angela*, first published in 1996, which is now in its fourth edition, and has sold 6,000 copies, mostly on local recommendation.

Another talented bridge-player and teacher, who was a member of both the West Kent and the Counties, and whose parents had been long-term members of both Clubs, was Peter Llewelyn-Jones. Peter had returned from the USA and, with Angela Tompson, he started the Alpha Club which met (with the agreement of the Counties' Committee) at the club-house on Thursday evenings. This was a "fun" club which provided classes for beginners with parties and other events, some of which were for the benefit of charities. Some of the youngsters progressed to EBU events and earned more "green" points for special events than "black" ones at the Club. Others, however, found themselves with less time to play after getting married and/or taking jobs in the City. A new generation of players was nonetheless encouraged by Peter and Angela, and many of them are members of the Club today. Chris Morgan and Lene Gook helped with the classes, and these arrangements continued until 2002.

1984

In 1984 the Counties Club's Committee took the decision to transfer the major part of the Club's bridge activities to the Centenary Room and the former ground floor Reading Room. This was to reduce the large heating bill and make life easier for members who found the stairs difficult. A room was also made available for a summer school for Italian students. The Committee also considered the possibility of selling the club-house and purchasing a large house or plot of land on the outskirts of the town, but this idea was not pursued.

Also in 1984 Dimmie Fleming was elected President of the Kent Contract Bridge Association. She had served for a long time on the KCBA's Committee which had benefitted greatly from the depth of her experience as an international player and as Secretary of the EBU for many years.

In the same year Scott Page [pictured overleaf] published his autobiography *Recollections of a Provincial Dental Surgeon* and presented Maud Corbett with a copy, inscribed "Hoping that it will bring back happy memories covering 50 years". Scott is remembered with affection by members of the Counties Club and the West Kent, who either played bridge with him or were amongst his patients.

1985

The Wellington Bridge Club

Ray White founded the Wellington Bridge Club, which started "life" at the Wellington Hotel, as a private club for friends of his who were experienced players, and in 1985 he arranged for its members' Friday evening duplicate sessions to be played at the club-house. There were usually 6-9 tables and amongst the players, in addition to Ray and Madeleine White, were Baroness Knoop, Elise Williams, Syd and Clare Shaw, John and Phyllis Lushington, Liz Gordon and Jean Smallwood. The arrangements were informal and there was no membership fee – the players paying only the required table money for each session. As the West Kent also had sessions on Friday evenings in the Centenary Room, there was a "buzz" in the Club, but unfortunately not enough space for all concerned to park their cars on the forecourt of the club-house.

Also in 1985 Jeremy Willans was elected to the Counties Club's Committee, and in 1989 he became Vice-Chairman. He played in the Club's Monday and Wednesday evening sessions and directed and scored many of these, and he also played in the West Kent's sessions on Tuesdays and Fridays, and in their teams. One of his regular partners was Baroness Olga Knoop who was pleased to take him under her wing. She was then residing at the Spa Hotel and would bring superior hotel sandwiches to the Club which she and Jeremy would consume before the duplicate sessions began. Jeremy also played in the Kent team throughout the 1980s and in 1987 he was appointed Captain. His team of eight has won the Tollemache Cup three times since 1980 and been runners-up a number of times. He qualified for the Philip Morris European Pairs in Paris in 1987, playing with Terry Goldsmith, and again in 1989 in Salsomaggiore Italy, playing with John Murrell. Amongst their opponents were Omar Sharif and Pietro Forquet (b.1925). The latter had, under his belt, 15 world championship titles with the Italian Blue Team.

Scott Page – c 1980

John & Phyllis Lushington in 1985 on their Diamond Wedding Anniversary

Ray White

In 1987 Ray White became Chairman of the Counties Club. He had been Chairman of the Kent Contract Bridge Association and had been running the bridge and the annual Summer Congress at the Club since the 1970s and he remained Chairman of the Club until 1998.

Ray White

It was a difficult time financially – in 1986 the boiler had to be replaced at a cost of £2,500 and the Club made a loss. Then the Club was informed by the Tunbridge Wells Council that its fire precautions were below standard, and was required to carry out building alterations for safety purposes and to renew its licence to sell alcohol. Paying for this work necessitated an increase in subscriptions and table money. In the following year, further significant expenditure was incurred re-furbishing the residential flat on the second floor.

At the end of 1989 the Counties Club had 109 Full Members and 90 Duplicate Members. Its financial position had improved somewhat as a result of a surplus of £1,489 after allocating £4,500 to pay for the re-wiring of the club-house.

22

1990 - 2004

Maud Corbett died in 1990. She had continued attending West Kent Committee meetings in her capacity as Life President until July 1988. She had devoted some 40 years to the West Kent Club, and to the Kent Contract Bridge Association, and is remembered with great affection by those who knew her.

Also in 1990, Lundie Rees, who had provided such good support to Maud in the 1960s, received a Dimmie Fleming Award for services to bridge in Somerset. His grandson, Jeremy Willans, played that year in a Kent team which included Gerald Soper and Terry Goldsmith in a challenge match at the club-house against the Great Britain Junior Team. His team lost, but honour was restored when Kent won the return match in the following year. In 1993, Jeremy won all three events at the 30th Anniversary of the Porthcawl Congress and in 1995 he reached the quarter final of the Gold Cup.

Catherine Draper had been taught bridge by her husband, Ian, a very successful player, in the late 1980s. She joined the West Kent and the Counties Club and played in local and county events, and served on the KCBA Committee for some 10 years from 1992. She was a member of one of the only two teams to win and retain the Pachabo Cup, and she has won numerous events including the Portland Pairs, the Garden Cities Trophy, the Autumn Congress Teams, the Jersey Swiss Pairs, the Easter Guardian and the Year-end Congress Teams.

Bridge-players were often heavy smokers in the early days – smoking was a habit which was very acceptable in social circles and it could also calm nerves at the bridge-table. However, by the 1990s, public opinion was moving against smoking in public places, and the debate extended to private clubs. Some smokers, though, regarded the pleasure of smoking as an "inalienable" right, and others agreed that this "right" should be preserved. At the AGM of the West Kent in 1992, a number of respected members resigned when a narrow majority of the members present voted to ban smoking during their bridge sessions. The Counties Club, whose members included some of the same people, was using the same premises on different days, and found an alternative solution which was to permit smoking during part of their sessions and/or in part of the room. Nonetheless, this issue remained contentious for a number of years in both Clubs.[102]

In about 1994 Diane Rogers, who had been teaching bridge in Tonbridge for some 10 years, started a regular session at the Club for beginners. She has enjoyed considerable success at the bridge table, in particular with the "colourful" and talented Eddie Lucioni, with whom she won the mixed pairs at Porthcawl; since 1998 she has taught bridge on P&O cruise ships.

John Lushington defied old age. After the death of his wife Phyllis, he lived in the Vale Royal Hotel (now the Smart and Simple Hotels) in London Road, and continued to thrive on his bridge. His playing partners would pick him up at the hotel and bring him to the Club where he was a virtual resident. He would play rubber bridge in the afternoon, enjoy a sandwich, and then play duplicate in the evening. His regular "North" seat would be reserved for him. He would

---

[102] Smoking was later prohibited in the club-house and then, on 1 July 2007, Government legislation made smoking unlawful in all Club premises

sometimes hire one of the rooms at the Club for a bridge session with some of his friends. John found this routine most agreeable, and kept it up until shortly before his death in 1995 at the age of 96.

One of John Lushington's playing partners was Dr Francis Briggs, who remembers him as "*a lovely man with great charm*". "*He was a skilful player and would ask 'dummy' to play the cards from the table (as in duplicate), and demonstrate a fine ability to play each hand in the most profitable way.*" Francis is a past captain of the Royal Ashdown Forest Golf Club, who after a busy career in medical practice, found time to play bridge. He served on the Committee of the Counties Club and organized the rubber bridge at the Club for a number of years in the 1990s.

Another past captain of the Royal Ashdown Forest Golf Club is Patrick Shovelton CB, CMG (b.1919), who had an illustrious career in the civil aviation and shipping industries and helped in the United Kingdom's entry negotiations into the European Economic Community in the 1970s. Patrick also served on the Counties Club's Committee in the 90s and, outside the Club, worked hard to protect the Tunbridge Wells Common; he still enjoys regular rubber bridge at his clubs in London.

In 1995 John Murrell, who was a member of both the West Kent and the Counties Club, was approached by Richard and Molly Burrows with a request that he should take over as Chairman of the West Kent. John had retired in 1992 after being Chief Executive at Gabitas Thring, the educational consultancy firm. He had played in a number of Gold Cups with Mike Griffiths, Jeremy Willans and Gerald Soper and with them he reached the semi-finals of the EBU Spring Fours at the Grand Hotel, Eastbourne. He also played rubber bridge at St James's Bridge Club and took up teaching bridge. John agreed to become Chairman of the West Kent on the understanding that he would devote his energies to bring about an amalgamation with the Counties Club. He restored the Club's original name, the West Kent Bridge Club, and held the office of Chairman for the next six years. He endeavoured, whenever the opportunity arose, to promote the idea of a merger. He also worked hard to promote the West Kent's sessions and introduced some new procedures for its club nights.

In 1996 Dimmie Fleming died. She had become a World Bridge Federation World Life Master and will be remembered as one of the country's leading lady players of her generation. Her memory is honoured by the annual Dimmie Fleming Awards made by the EBU to individuals for services to county bridge. Her former bridge-partner, Vida Bingham, was elected to the Committee of the West Kent in 1996 and served on it until 2004. Nigel Osmer became Vida's regular bridge partner and in 2001 they won the EBU Veterans Pairs Championship.

In 1998 Colin Wilson was elected Chairman of the KCBA and held that office until 2003. Diana Avis became his regular bridge partner and they won the South East final of the Hubert Phillips Cup (playing with Jeremy Willans and Gerald Soper) and the Silver Plate (with Pat Reardon and Richard Pengelly) and the Swiss teams event (twice) at the EBU Seniors Congress in Eastbourne. Colin has won all the major Kent trophies and has particularly enjoyed competing in the Hunter Homines (Men's Pairs), winning this event some five times with Jeremy Willans. He now gives master classes at the Club.

Also in 1998 Ray White retired after 11 years as Chairman of the Counties Club (which had by then added the word "Bridge" to its name and became the Tunbridge Wells and Counties Bridge Club), although he continued as Treasurer.

Helen Sanders, the head of the Tunbridge Wells Land Registry, was elected to succeed Ray as Chairman – not an easy task, but she brought her professional skill and experience to the role.

In 1999 Ethnie Hodgens became Chairman. She had been the first lay Headmistress of the Cavendish School in Camden Town. She had served on the Counties Club's Committee for several years, having first joined the Club as a country member in 1970, and she had also served on the West Kent's Committee from 1989-92. She does not claim to be as good a player as her mother, Vera, but she enjoys rubber bridge and has won the Lushington Trophy three times since 1997. Ethnie was assisted by Mary Pritchard, who became Club Secretary, and Jean Smallwood, who kept the books.

2000

In 2000 the Counties Club's President, the 5th Marquess of Abergavenny died. His nephew, Christopher George Charles Nevill (b.1955), the son of his younger brother Lord Rupert Nevill CVO, DL, JP (1923-1982) succeeded to the title of the 6th Marquess of Abergavenny. The Club was most honoured when he agreed to become its second President.

In August of that year, John Murrell, the Chairman of the West Kent, reported to the Committee that he had made a preliminary approach to the Chairman of the Counties regarding a possible merger between the two clubs. In the following month the West Kent Committee held a special meeting to consider a proposal drafted by a working party consisting of two members of the Counties and two members of the West Kent for a closer relationship between the several clubs which played bridge at 40 London Road. However the West Kent Committee felt that an amalgamation would be inappropriate, largely it seems because they wished to preserve the identity and ethos of the West Kent. Nonetheless they wanted to continue playing bridge at the club-house and, recognising that the Counties lacked the resources necessary to maintain the building, agreed to listen carefully to their approaches.

In November the Counties Club held a Special General Meeting at which it was agreed to create a single class of members and a flat rate of membership subscription – everyone would pay an annual subscription of £20 – instead of Full Members paying £22.85 and Duplicate Members about half that amount. All members would be entitled to vote at General Meetings and share in the ownership of the Club's assets. This rationalisation of the Counties' membership structure was a desirable step towards facilitating a merger between the Counties and the West Kent - not only by creating a single class of membership, but also by extending the franchise to all members.

In 2001 the Counties Club's Committee, mindful of the need to improve the Club's finances, required the West Kent players (who were not also members of the Counties Club) to pay a surcharge of 50 pence each on their table money per session – this to be set aside to meet the cost of maintenance of the club-house. Robert Beveridge succeeded John Murrell as Chairman of the West Kent.

In 2002 Stephen Pierce (who had joined the Counties Club in 1997) succeeded Ethnie Hodgens as Chairman, and Ethnie was elected a Life Member. Monica Aitken took over the running of the Club's annual Congress with considerable success, although numbers (as at other bridge events) were beginning to wane.

Stephen had played bridge at school and university, although chess was his favourite game. He started playing bridge again at the Tonbridge Bridge Club in 1991, joined the West Kent in 1993 and was Chairman of the Tonbridge Club from 1996-2001. He shared the view of John Murrell and others that the time had come for the Counties Club, the West Kent, and the Wellington Club to become a single club. Their respective members had, after all, been playing the same game in the same place for some 20 years. Stephen established a working party of four, Tom Pigott and himself representing the Counties and Robert Beveridge and Brian Lippard representing the West Kent; they discussed the financial and other aspects of an amalgamation. The West Kent name would no longer be used, but its competitions and traditions would be preserved. Ray White, Peggy Heilbron, Kaia Bell, Jean Paxton, Diana Avis, Yvonne Bowman, and Peter Nicholls looked into the bridge-related aspects of the proposed merger, including the co-ordination of the calendar and competitions and directors' and scorers' rotas.

In 2003 (the year before he died) Ray White was elected President of the KCBA and in October of that year he was presented at the EBU's AGM with the Dimmie Fleming Award for services to bridge in Kent.

2004

On 9 February 2004 after more than 12 months of discussions, Stephen Pierce circulated to the Counties Club's members the terms and conditions of the proposed merger with the West Kent Bridge Club. He stated that Ray White, on behalf of the Wellington Bridge Club, had indicated that, should a merger take place, the Wellington would not operate as a separate club within the building on Friday nights. As it was a proprietary club, it would not be part of the merger so far as voting was concerned, but it would be treated as part of the combined club.[103] No recommendations were made regarding the merger and members of the Counties and the West Kent would be asked to make up their own minds how to vote. There would be a special meeting on 6 March for questions and answers about the merger but no discussion, and members would be required to register their votes for or against the merger by 12 March.

The Counties Club had 325 members, of whom 100 were also members of the West Kent. The West Kent had 150 members, ie including 50 who were not members of the Counties Club, and Stephen stated that up to 25 of those were expected to leave if the merger was approved. There were anomalies as regards the annual subscriptions because members of the Counties Club paid £35, West Kent members paid £10 only and those who were members of both clubs paid £45.

The perceived advantages of the merger were that the assets of the clubs would be pooled and everybody playing club level bridge would contribute equally to the upkeep and maintenance of the building (paying an annual subscription of £35) irrespective of the sessions in which they played. Joint members would save £10 in membership fees, there would be a single focused club, simplified financial and administrative arrangements, opportunities for a club website, increased levels of competitions and scope for promoting rubber bridge, and members would have the opportunity to choose their playing sessions without changing clubs. The only perceived disadvantages were the loss of the West Kent's identity and the potential loss of revenue from those West Kent members who left or stopped playing at the Club.

The merger was approved separately by the majority of the members of both clubs, and this result was announced at the AGM of the Counties Club on 30 April. The West Kent transferred its investments of some £8,000 to the Counties Club, and those members of the West Kent who

---

[103] All the Wellington's members had a vote by virtue of their membership of the Counties Club

were not already members of the Counties became members of the combined club (unless they wished to leave) and acquired an immediate share in the ownership of its assets. The Counties Club then changed its name to the Tunbridge Wells Bridge Club.

POSTSCRIPT

Since the merger in 2004 the Club's membership has increased to about 400. It is a sign of the times that a flat television screen now shows the computerized running scores at each of the Club's eight weekly duplicate sessions. These cover all levels of ability, and there are also sessions of rubber bridge and chicago, and bridge classes.

Andrew Robson, bridge correspondent of The Times, winner of a European Championship, back to back Gold Cups and many other major events, and one of the country's leading bridge players, teachers and writers, has visited the Club twice to give master classes.

In 2005, Jeremy Willans and Catherine Draper (who now lives in Lancashire) played for England in the Camrose Cup matches against Wales and the Republic of Ireland. In 2008 Catherine was in the team which won the Lady Milne Trophy, took part in the European Championships in Pau and won a Gold Medal playing for the British Ladies team in the Beijing Mind Games Olympics. In 2009, Jeremy has won the Brighton Swiss Teams and the new Premier Grand Masters event, Colin Wilson and Diana Avis have won the Premier Kent Pairs Championship, and Vida Bingham and Nigel Osmer have won the Sussex Congress Mixed Pairs.

Jeremy Willans and Catherine Draper
in their England shirts for the 2005 Camrose Cup

The club-house is one of the nine current venues in England for the annual Portland Pairs event (the EBU National Mixed Pairs championship). The Centenary of the building will be marked by the 50th Congress of the Kent Contract Bridge Association (founded by John Westall Pearson and his daughter Maud Corbett) which will take place at the club-house at the end of October - followed in November by a week of special events to mark the Centenary of the Counties Club's occupation of the building. These will include the annual competition for the Lushington Cup (celebrating rubber bridge - "the pure game") and a new competition for a trophy presented by the immediate past Chairman, Brian Forty.

Finally, congratulations to Vida Bingham on the success of her horse, Mon Mome, which on 4 April 2009 won the Grand National, the world's most famous horserace. Steeplechasing was the passion of Lord "Dashalong" Sefton (the father of the Club's Founder Member and first Trustee, the Hon Francis Molyneux) who provided the racecourse at Aintree and laid its Foundation Stone. It is fitting that a horse owned by a member of the Club should win this prestigious event this year and with a starting price of 100-1. If Francis had been watching in the stands, might he have enjoyed a wager even more profitable than Phileas Fogg's?

SELECTED BIBLIOGRAPHY

Aldous, Richard, *The Lion and the Unicorn*, Hutchinson, 2006

Bassett, Roger W, *Better Then Than Now – A History of Tunbridge Wells Rangers Football Club and Tunbridge Wells F.C. (Two Blues)*, Greenman Enterprise, 2008

Cardus, Neville, *Good Days*, 1934

Cobb, Richard, *Still Life – Sketches from a Tunbridge Wells Childhood*, Chatto & Windus, 1983

Cunningham, John, *400 Years of The Wells*, Royal Tunbridge Wells Civic Society, 2005

Cunningham, John, *The Origins of Warwick Park and the Nevill Ground*, Royal Tunbridge Wells Civic Society, 2007

Dalton, William, *Complete Bridge*, Frederick A Stokes, New York, 1900

Elers, Frederick Wadham, *The Tunbridge Wells General Hospital*, Pelton, c. 1910

Eliot, George, *Middlemarch*, 1871

Fleming, Ian, *Moonraker*, 1955

Francis, Henry G, *The Official Encyclopedia of Bridge (6th Edition)*, ACBL Inc, 2001

Graves, Charles, *Leather Armchairs – The Chivas Regal book of London Clubs*, Cassell & Co Ltd, 1963

Hasenson, Peter, *British Bridge Almanac*, 77 Publishing, 2004

Jones, Chris, *Tunbridge Wells in 1909*, Royal Tunbridge Wells Civic Society, 2008

Knipe, Henry R, *Nebula to Man*, J M Dent, 1905

Lamb, Charles, *Essays of Elia*, 1821

Major, John, *More than a Game – The Story of Cricket's Early Years*, HarperCollins, 2007

Macleod, Iain, *Bridge is an Easy Game*, Frederick Muller, 1952

Nicolson, Juliet, *The Perfect Summer – Dancing into Shadow in 1911*, John Murray, 2006

Nevill, Ralph, *London Clubs*, Chatto & Windus, 1911

Page, G Scott, *Recollections of a Provincial Dental Surgeon*, Casdec Ltd., 1984

Peacock, David, *Tunbridge Wells Sketchbook* (text by Frank Chapman), Perspective Press, 1978

Poe, Edgar Allan, *The Murders in the Rue Morgue*, 1841

Porter, Roger, *The Forest Row Golf Club*

Reese, Terence, *Story of an Accusation*, Chess & Bridge Ltd 2004 edition

Reffell Family History, www.reffell.org.uk

Savidge, Alan, *Royal Tunbridge Wells*, Midas Books, 1975

Thomson, J Radford, *Pelton's Illustrated Guide to Tunbridge Wells*, Pelton, 1883

Truscott, Alan, *The Great Bridge Scandal*, Master Point Press, 2004 edition

Truscott, Alan and Dorothy, *The New York Times Bridge Book*, St Martin's Press, 2002

Verne, Jules, *Around the World in 80 Days*, 1872

The Kent and Sussex Courier

The Tunbridge Wells Gazette

Tunbridge Wells Society

The Advertiser

CHAIRMEN OF THE TUNBRIDGE WELLS AND COUNTIES CLUB – TUNBRIDGE WELLS BRIDGE CLUB

1908 Henry Knipe	1967 Brig E Dangerfield	1998 Miss Helen Sanders
1918 Col Alfred Simpson	1968 Harold Shuter	1999 Miss Ethnie Hodgens
1934 Frank Weare	1970 Harold Cowen	2002 Stephen Pierce
1941 Neville Stone	1974 Mrs Daphne Lee	2006 Oliver Kinsey
1943 Dr Trustram Watson	1975 R Searle	2007 Brian Forty
1951 A J Mitchell	1977 Ronald Halfhead	2009 Brian Lippard
1956 Brig Geoffrey Hall	1987 Ray White	

CHAIRMEN OF THE WEST KENT BRIDGE CLUB AFTER THE SALE OF 12 BOYNE PARK

1972 Vic Drew

1973 Richard Warner

1989 Ken Thomas

1992 Brian Ping

1993 Peter Harrold

1995 John Murrell

2001 Robert Beveridge

THE NUMBER OF TWC/TWCC/TWBC MEMBERS

1886	118	1958	172	1974	540 [inc Squash]
1930	180	1964	145	1975	270
1941	126	1969	171	1980	255
1946	117	1970	208	2002	300
1949	204	1972	602 [inc Squash]	2004	325
				2009	400

INDEX

Abergavenny, Marquesses of. *See* Nevill
Adams, Bill, 93
Aitken, Monica, 100
Allington, Rev H G, 19
Alpha Club, 95
Andrews, Lawford, 58
Ashburnham, Lady Georgiana, 7
Ashton, E R, 58
Avis, Diana, 94, 99, 101, 103
Bartram, George, 19
Beale, Louis Stephen, 26, 27, 30, 31, 33, 37, 51
Bell, Kaia, 101
Bentinck, Lord Henry, 21
Beveridge, Robert, 100, 101, 105
Billiards, 1, 5, 19, 45, 51, 54, 56, 58, 60, 61, 66, 73, 74, 79
Bingham, Vida, 86, 92, 93, 99, 103
Blackwell, Pauline, 66, 83
Botham, Ian, 94
Bowman, Yvonne, 95, 101
Bowne, General Lord, 77
Brennan, Lady, 83
Bretherton, Gordon, 58
Briggs, Dr Francis, 99
Buller, Lt Col Walter, 46, 48, 59
Burns, Cecil, 30, 33
Burrows, Major Richard, 90, 95, 99
Burrows, Molly, 90, 91, 95, 99
Burton, Decimus, 5, 13
Canning, George, 4th Lord Harris, 10, 43
Carlton Club, 4
Chipperfield, Miss D, 84
Clay, James, 21
Cobb, Diana, 61
Cobb, Richard, 25, 52, 53, 54, 61
Cohen, Ben, 50
Collinson, John, 22, 23
Corbett, Maud, 44, 49, 53, 62, 66, 67, 70, 74, 75, 77, 78, 84, 86, 87, 89, 90, 94, 95, 98, 103
Corbett, Rex, 59, 62, 74, 75, 78, 86, 87, 90
Cowen, Harold, 73, 79, 80, 81, 105
Cripps, William Charles, 51, 58, 64
Crompton, Mrs, 66, 74
Culbertson, Ely, 44, 47, 48, 50, 52, 54, 65, 86
Currie, Mr and Mrs, 59
Dangerfield, Brig E P, 73, 105
Dillon, Jo, 44, 48

Disraeli, Benjamin, 4, 15, 16
Dixon, James Frederick, 45, 59, 65
Draper, Catherine, 98, 103
Dredge, Mrs, 79
Drew, Vic, 88, 105
Drummond, Pauline, 61
Dutton, Sir Frederick, 47
Dymant, Dai, 83
Elers, Frederick Wadham, 7, 9, 10, 19, 38, 39, 43
English Bridge Union, 50, 55, 63, 66, 70, 81, 88, 89, 91, 94, 95, 99, 101
Fleming, Dimmie, 50, 52, 59, 61, 62, 70, 75, 76, 77, 78, 84, 86, 88, 92, 93, 95, 98, 99, 101
Fleming, Ian, 64
Fleming, Leslie, 50, 52, 61, 70, 77, 78, 84, 86, 93
Fletcher Lutwidge, Major C R, 7, 10, 19, 26, 43
Forty, Brian, 103, 105
Foster, Sir John, 77
Gardener, Nico, 64
Gibbons, Mary, 61
Gilbert, Daphne, 75, 78, 90, 92, 94
Gladstone, William, 4
Glubb, John, 82, 83, 91, 94
Gold Cup, 49, 52, 59, 63, 64, 70, 75, 84, 85, 98, 99, 103
Goldsmid, Sir Julian, 7, 8, 16
Goldsmith, Terry, 94, 96, 98
Gook, Lene, 94, 95
Gordon, Fritzi, 64, 76
Gordon, John, 30, 31
Gordon, Liz, 96
Grace, W G, 10, 38, 43
Great Hall, 7, 8, 17, 39, 60, 74
Griffiths, Mike, 78, 82, 83, 84, 85, 93, 94, 99
Guest, Capel, 73, 74, 75, 77, 79, 87, 89
Guest, Joan, 73, 74, 79
Hailstone, Bernard, 65
Halfhead, Ronald, 84, 91, 92, 105
Hall, Brig Geoffrey, 58, 60, 65, 74, 81, 105
Hall, Christopher, 65, 84, 95
Hallward, Mr, 64
Hanson, David, 59
Harding-Edgar, Mrs, 86
Harries, Frank Shearme, 58
Harrison-Gray, Maurice, 50, 52, 72, 75, 76
Harrold, Peter, 105
Harvey, Eric, 49, 52

Harvey, John, 67, 70
Harvey, Maud, 52
Harvey, Michael, 67, 70
Heilbron, Peggy, 101
Hempson, Mrs, 48
Hill, Diana, 82, 83, 94
Hill, Phyllis Irene, 50
Hodgens, Ethnie, 61, 67, 100, 105
Hodgens, Vera, 61, 100
Hoyle, Edmund, 21
Hunt, Ann, 67
Ives, Mona, 94
Jacoby, Oswald, 48, 64
Johnson, Dr John, 14, 19
Johnston, James, 94
Jones, Henry ("Cavendish"), 21, 24
Jones, Henry Derviche, 21
Juan, Jane, 76
Kempson, Ewart, 77
Kent and Sussex Club, 39, 60, 74
Kent Contract Bridge Association, 1, 53, 55, 62, 66, 70, 75, 77, 80, 87, 91, 94, 95, 98, 99, 101
Kerin, Dorothy, 71
Kingsland, Mike, 91, 93, 94
Kinsey, Oliver, 105
Kirk, Alexandra, 39, 40, 42
Kirk-Greene, Helen, 52, 61
Kirk-Greene, Leslie, 61
Knipe, Henry Robert, 27, 28, 30, 31, 37, 42, 105
Knoop, Baron Alexander, 41, 71
Knoop, Baroness Olga, 41, 52, 59, 61, 71, 78, 84, 85, 96
Konstam, Kenneth, 59, 60, 76
Langridge, Mrs, 83
Langridge, Walter, 83
Leate, Squadron Leader D S, 80
Lee, Daphne, 74, 82, 84, 89, 105
Lenz, Sidney, 48, 64
Lewis, Trixie, 52, 61
Limbery-Buse, Geoffrey, 53
Limbery-Buse, Richard, 25, 44, 51, 53, 54, 55, 56
Lippard, Brian, 82, 84, 85, 91, 93, 101, 105
Llewelyn-Jones, Peter, 95
Lott, John, 66, 70, 75
Lott, Ralph, 66
Lucas, Rear Admiral Charles, 28, 29
Lucioni, Eddie, 98
Lushington, James Law, 24, 81
Lushington, John, 24, 67, 81, 83, 85, 91, 96, 98
Lushington, Percy Manners, 24
Lushington, Phyllis, 50, 81, 83, 96, 98

Macleod, Iain, 50
Manser, Dr Frederick, 12, 45, 56
Markus, Rixi, 60, 64, 76, 77, 92
Marsack, Dr B, 12
Marx, Jack, 50, 52
Mathieson, Graham, 59
Matthews, Sir John Bromhead, 45, 48
McCausland, Mr, 44
McClean, Frank, 12
McClean, Sir Francis, 13, 32
McDowell, T, 65
Mills, Anne, 84, 93
Millson, Betty, 87, 90
Millson, Douglas, 87, 90
Mitchell, A J, 64, 105
Molyneux, Hon Francis George, 7, 8, 19, 20, 103
Morgan, Chris, 95
Morland, Charles William, 14
Moss, Mary, 76
Mr and Mrs Handley, 84
Murrell, John, 75, 78, 84, 93, 96, 99, 100, 105
Murton, Sir Walter, 38
Murton-Neale, Douglas, 58
Nettleton, Heather, 24, 67, 81
Nevill Ground, 16, 20, 26, 43
Nevill, Christopher, 6th M. of Abergavenny, 100
Nevill, Hon George, 15
Nevill, Lady Joan, 37, 45
Nevill, Lord Henry, 15, 37, 43, 45
Nevill, Lord Richard, 45
Nevill, Sir John, 5th M. of Abergavenny, 80, 83
Nevill, Sir William, 1st M. of Abergavenny, 15, 43
Nicholls, Peter, 101
Nicolaidi, Michael Panioti, 41
Nutting, Kathleen, 52
Oettinger, Bridget, 82
Osmer, Nigel, 99, 103
Oswald-Smith, Audrey, 52, 61, 63
Page, George Scott, 49, 52, 61, 66, 67, 70, 75, 78, 80, 84, 85, 95
Palmer, Peggy, 78, 83, 85, 87, 92
Parker, Captain Edward, 59
Paxton, Jean, 101
Pearson, Dorothy, 44, 49, 50, 52, 60, 66
Pearson, John Westall, 44, 49, 50, 52, 53, 59, 60, 61, 62, 63, 64, 66, 103
Pengelly, Richard, 91, 99
Picton, Alan, 79
Picton, Dulcinora, 79, 80, 84
Pierce, Stephen, 100, 101, 105
Piercy, Rev H M, 73

Pigott, Tom, 80, 101
Ping, Brian, 94, 105
Portland Club, 5, 21, 23, 24, 31, 47, 57, 64
Pratt, Lord George, 18
Pratt, Sir John, 4th Marquess Camden, 37, 45
Preston, Charles, 59
Price, Amy, 67
Pritchard, Mary, 100
Puckle, H C, 19
Quinton, Peter, 82, 84, 85
Rayne, Edward, 60
Reardon, Pat, 99
Recaldin, Mr, 91
Rees, Lundie, 77, 78, 87, 91, 98
Reese, Anne, 47, 61
Reese, Terence, 47, 50, 59, 63, 75, 76, 77
Reich, David, 89, 90, 91
Reily, Charles, 14, 19
Rhodes, Doris Lady, 60
Rhodes, Rev H J, 14
Richard, Freda, 91, 94
Richardson, Sheila, 80
Rigby, Kevin, 94
Robson, Andrew, 77, 103
Rogers, Diane, 98
Royal Ashdown Forest Golf Club, 38, 45, 99
Salomons, Sir David Lionel, 10, 11, 16, 43, 58
Sanders, Helen, 100, 105
Schapiro, Boris, 59, 63, 75, 77
Scott, Archdeacon Avison T, 11, 38, 45
Sealy, May, 78
Searle, R, 105
Seeckts, Robert, 81, 82
Sefton, Lord "Dashalong", 7, 103
Shanahan, Dorothy, 76
Sharif, Omar, 85, 96
Shaw, Clare, 85, 96
Shaw, Sir John Charles Kenward, 18
Shaw, Syd, 85, 96
Shelford (Steward), 56
Shelford, William, 56
Sherriff Charles, W, 55
Shovelton, Patrick, 99
Shuter, Harold, 74, 105
Sidney, Algernon, Lord de L'Isle, 45
Simon, Seca Jascha "Skid", 50, 52
Simpson, Colonel Alfred Thomas, 9, 20, 26, 27, 31, 37, 39, 40, 42, 43, 50, 59, 105
Simpson, Sir Maurice, 58
Simpson, Thomas Fox, 7, 8, 11, 20, 26, 59

Smallwood, Jean, 96, 100
Smith, Apsley, 19
Snape, Charles, 95
Soper, Gerald, 82, 84, 85, 93, 98, 99
Spratt, Lt Jack, 14
Spratt, Rear Admiral Thomas, 14, 18
Squash, 1, 37, 51, 56, 60, 67, 74, 79, 80, 81, 82, 83, 84, 105
Starling, Dr Cyril, 61
Starling, Nancy, 61
Stone, Canon, 48
Stone, Frank William, 7, 8, 11, 19, 43, 56, 59
Stone, Neville, 12, 56, 57, 59, 105
Stone-Wigg, John, 7, 9, 58
Swimer, Ralph, 77
Swinnerton–Dyer, Peter, 70
Tatlow, Major Basil, 50, 82, 86
Thomas, Ken, 105
Thomson, Douglas, 79, 80, 81
Thornton, Caroline, 80
Thornton, Rev R T, 19
Tompson, Angela, 94, 95
Tremlett, Rear Admiral Francisco, 18
Truscott, Alan, 21, 64, 77, 92
Trustram Watson, Dr G, 57, 58, 60, 105
Tyrwhitt-Drake, E, 75, 78
Tyrwhitt-Drake, Mrs, 83
Vale Royal Bridge Club, 73
van Raalte, J, 31
Vanderbilt, Harold Stirling, 46
Ward, Arthur Wellesley, 13
Warner, Richard, 73, 78, 84, 88, 91, 92, 95, 105
Waters, Bernie, 67, 77, 80, 82, 83, 93
Weare, Frank, 51, 56, 105
Welch, Richard, 85, 93
Wellington Bridge Club, 95, 101
White, Madeleine, 75, 78, 80, 84, 87, 96
White, Ray, 75, 78, 80, 82, 84, 87, 88, 89, 91, 93, 94, 95, 96, 97, 99, 101, 105
Whitelaw Cup, 60, 88, 92
Willans, Jeremy, 84, 91, 93, 94, 96, 98, 99, 103
Williams, Elise, 89, 94, 96
Wilson, Colin, 93, 94, 99, 103
Winterscale, Colonel J F M, 40
Witt, Mrs D M, 65, 66
Wix, Samuel, 19
Woods, David, 91
Woolley, Frank, 43, 94
Young-Hughes, Eleanor, 52, 61